BLACK GENEALOGY

BLACK
GENEA

PRENTICE-HALL, INC., Englewood Cliffs, New Jersey

Charles L. Blockson
with Ron Fry

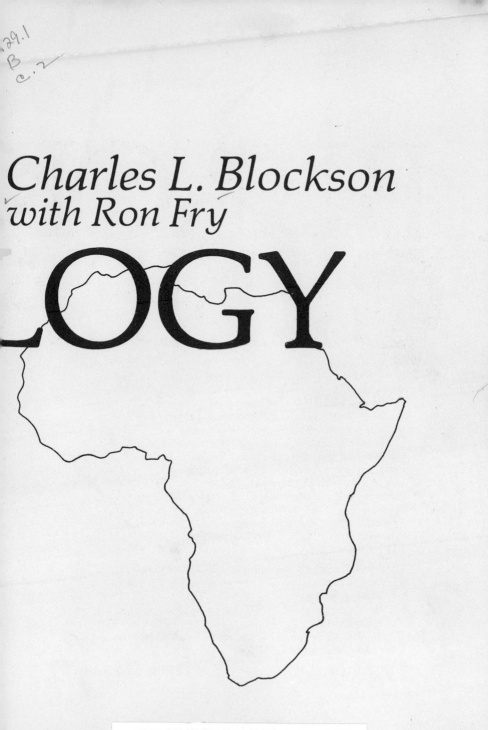

LOGY

Printed in the United States of America
Prentice-Hall International, Inc., London
Prentice-Hall of Australia, Pty. Ltd., Sydney
Prentice-Hall of Canada, Ltd., Toronto
Prentice-Hall of India Private Ltd., New Delhi
Prentice-Hall of Japan, Inc., Tokyo
Prentice-Hall of Southeast Asia Pte. Ltd., Singapore
Whitehall Books Limited, Wellington, New Zealand
10 9 8 7 6 5 4 3 2 1

Library of Congress Cataloging in Publication Data
Blockson, Charles L
    Black genealogy.
    Bibliography: p.
    Includes index.
    1. Afro-Americans—Genealogy—Handbooks, manuals, etc.
I. Fry, Ron, joint author. II. Title.
CS21.B55   929'.1'028   77-3150
ISBN 0-13-077685-8

To Mother Africa
and to five of her most
illustrious children

Toussaint L'Ouverture
Frederick Douglass
Harriet Tubman
Paul Robeson
&
Alex Haley

Acknowledgements

I am indebted to many persons for their assistance in making this book possible.

I am deeply indebted to Dr. James E. Mooney, director of the Historical Society of Pennsylvania, and his staff for giving me access to their excellent collection of manuscripts.

To the staff of Delaware Hall of Records, Dover, Delaware, for their gracious hospitality and for providing me with documents pertaining to the white Blockson family.

The staff of the Newport, Rhode Island, Historical Society and the staff of the Montgomery County Library, Norristown, Pennsylvania, were generous with their time and offered many helpful suggestions.

It probably will be impossible to pay tribute to all who have helped to make this book become reality; however, I am indebted to the following persons who provided me with encouragement and advised me during the past ten years: my family; Mr. Raymond Trent of the University of Pennsylvania's Biddle Law Library; Dr. Cyril E. Griffith, Department of History, Pennsylvania State University; Mrs. Katherine Baxter of the Council for Interracial Children's Books, New York City; Mrs. Brenda Saddler, Mrs. Alsa Cotner, Francine Ambandos, Frances Lambert, Northern Illinois University; Mr. Clarence L. Holte, noted Afro-American book collector, for making available for my use the rare Liberian census report; and to Pennsylvania State Representative Robert J. Butera, for listening patiently to my views on black history for the past twenty years.

Contents

Chapter One

THE CHALLENGE WE FACE

"Why can't I know my birthday?" Frederick Douglass asked as a child. The question revealed his yearnings to know not only his age, but also his background. Where did he come from? Who was his father? Who were his relatives?

Frederick Douglass was born a slave, around 1817. And though I was born a free man, over a hundred years later, I have to admit I too hung my head in shame because some of my white friends could trace their families back to William the Conqueror. I probably wasn't the only black who wished he could do that.

Two major factors have led to a growing interest in black genealogy. The first is a direct result of the great surge of black consciousness raising produced by the Civil Rights Movement of the 1960's. Blacks are now proud to wear dashikis and learn Swahili and be able to admit that their ancestors were bought and sold.

The grass-roots movement has produced two important and stimulating works thus far: Alex Haley's *Roots*, the true account of his own family's journey through history, and the fictionalized *Autobiography of Miss Jane Pittman*. Televised adaptations of both have heightened their impact on the black population. But any black American with an honest desire to trace his ancestry needs this book—if only to learn about the countless problems he's likely to run into.

Most genealogists are white men who specialize in tracing other white families back through history. Their clients pay dearly for such expertise, especially since a properly constructed family tree can take years to complete.

For those whites with a lot of money, too little time, and only a casual interest in the eventual results, hiring such a specialist is probably a good idea and a solid

investment. The genealogists are unusually proficient
in a number of record-searching disciplines and often
experts in some obscure field like heraldic blazonings or
family crests. For those willing to pay but unwilling
to undertake any of the drudgery themselves, such a
scholarly type is invaluable.

These experts *could* still be immensely helpful to a
black family seriously interested in tracing its ancestry.
But unfortunately, they probably *won't* be. Part of the
reason is basic economics—most of us could never
afford to pay for the years of work a really detailed
chart might require. But a more telling reason is purely
professional—any researcher tracing a black family tree
is faced with distinct and unique problems that he just
doesn't have to consider when tracing a white family's
ancestry.

Over the years, many important records, absolutely
necessary for any complete study of the black historical
experience, have been lost or destroyed. For example,
almost no information now exists on the hundreds of
beneficial societies blacks created during the nineteenth
century. Many of the thousands of churches, fraternal
organizations, and literary societies that flourished have
left nothing behind. The forced mobility of the black
community throughout the last two centuries only
deepens the problem.

Slavery, the bond we share, set up its own system of
hurdles—such as the enforced illiteracy of most slaves.
Although court, military, and other records can help
establish some of the basic data on an illiterate ancestor,
the lack of his *own* written clues make it especially
difficult to fill in the more human aspects of his life.
(I can recall that my own grandfather signed his name
with an X. As a child I took little notice of this; to me

he seemed an educated man.) A series of such setbacks due to illiteracy will make each new detail of the puzzle even more important and prized.

The frequent back-door sexual liaisons between black slaves and their white masters adds to the confusion. Were the resulting children ever recorded in official records? Often they were not or were simply entered after the mother's name as "infant."

Many names of slaves and free blacks were of a classical sort—Scipio or Caesar, Pompey or Cato— sometimes given in jest by a master who named his slaves in the same manner he might name a pet cat or dog. In many instances the person used only his first name or simply added the master's family name, all but obliterating any trace of his true heritage. If sold off at a later age, slaves were often rechristened by their new masters. In a series of sales over the years, M'chiba might become Cato, then Caesar, then George or Little Buck.

Finally, when freed, blacks themselves frequently threw off their slave names and adopted whatever "free" names they fancied, producing a flood of George Washingtons and Thomas Jeffersons. And Aunt Bessie, who "passed" so successfully at the turn of the century, probably constructed a wall of name and address changes essential to maintaining her "white" status. Such a maze of changes can drive even a professional genealogist up the nearest wall.

Worse yet, until recently, blacks were often denied access to the few extensive collections that do exist. In his book *Black Boy*, Richard Wright describes the difficulty he faced as a teenager trying to obtain books from the public library in Memphis, Tennessee. Blacks were simply not allowed to use its facilities unless they were in the building on errands for white men.

"Which of them whites [with whom he worked]," he wondered, "would now help me to get books? And how could I read them without causing [them] concern? . . . I had so far been successful in hiding my thoughts and feelings from them, but I knew that I would create hostility if I went about this business of reading in a clumsy way."

When Wright finally asked one of the whites if he could borrow his library card, the man agreed but warned that he mustn't let any of the other white men know what he was doing. To use the library, Richard took the card and a forged note, ostensibly from its owner.

"Dear Madam," he addressed the librarian, "Will you please let this nigger boy [I used the word 'nigger' to make the librarian feel that I could not possibly be the author of the note] have some books by H. L. Mencken?"

Until recently, groups like the Daughters of the American Revolution and Sons or Daughters of the Confederacy denied blacks access to any of their records. This was especially hard to stomach in the case of the Mormon Church, which a black man helped found, and which has the most extensive genealogical collection in the country. Just as the doors of supposedly public facilities have been closed to us, so have historical landmarks. Our ancestors' labor built and maintained places like Mount Vernon and Colonial Williamsburg. Yet today, these institutions mention slavery only in an occasional oblique reference to "servants" on the grounds.

Such intellectual segregation has severely restricted the search for black family ties. We've always been told by *others* what our past was like. Sociologists and psychologists—usually white—studied us and reported on us, but always seemed to concentrate on the pathological aspects of black family life. My lifelong interest in history helped me to avoid the destructiveness of this prevailing image. I knew that we had a culture and past to be proud of. Finally, I set out on a very personal mission to prove that contention through my own family's history.

In my own ten-year search for roots, I have had to confront all the obstacles you will face. I discovered that actually tracing an ancestor brought to America in chains requires an extensive search through breeding, plantation, and other slave records—if they can be located, for many are gone forever. If you're lucky enough to trace that slave back to the dock, finding the ship that transported him from Africa is an even greater problem. And the final steps—tracing that ship back to the African coastal slave factories and their barracoons (large corrals where blacks were kept like so many cattle) and from there to a particular African country and one of hundreds of tribes—are the hardest of all.

THE LUCK FACTOR

But despite all these obstacles, it *is* possible to obtain a lot of information in a relatively short time. And the luck factor is always hovering close by just to keep it interesting. One friend of mine, after hours of slogging through boxes of family relics, found an old photograph album. He was tempted just to lay it aside, but luckily he thumbed through it first. It turned out to be his great-grandmother's. In that one album, he found enough information to trace *seven* generations, all the way back to Savannah, Georgia, in 1795.

While working on this book, I had a personal stroke of luck. I found a 102-year-old relative living in Delaware. Minerva Blockson, born August 30, 1874, was a treasure house of information.

I asked her if she could recall certain members of my family. She said, "Let me focus my mind." It was interesting to note that she could remember things long ago more clearly than recent events. This is something for you to remember when you're interviewing elderly people—for it is a common phenomenon.

As I repeated names, she began to remember, and could recall names, births, deaths, marriages, and other events around Seaford and Bridgeville. Often mention of one event would trigger off other memories. When I questioned her about slavery, she paused and said, "The older black folk used to send the children away when they talked about slavery because they didn't want us to hear it."

Minerva Blockson's maternal grandfather was white, her parents black. She said it was common for white men to sire black children in those days. Her parents had both been slaves; but her actual grandfather was her parents' master. Her mother then gave her up, and Minerva was raised by the white family.

One of her most vivid memories concerned tales of Patty Cannon, a notorious slave catcher who had a house in Seaford in the late 1700's and early 1800's. She was noted for her cruel treatment of slaves, torturing and even murdering them. Minerva Blockson, as a child, was told never to go near her house.

She heard tales of several blacks who had escaped on the Underground Railroad (which she called "the Freedom Train") from the rural area of Delaware. She could recall the older folks changing their names after emancipation. Some took the name "Freeman" because

of their freedom, some took the name "Lincoln" after
the president, and others took the name "Douglass"
after Frederick Douglass, who was born in Tuckahoe,
Maryland.

Mrs. Blockson said that in earlier times the black
section of town was referred to as Colored Town. Yet,
when I first arrived in Bridgeville in August 1976 and
asked for Mrs. Minerva Blockson, I was told she lived
in Colored Town. The name has not yet disappeared.

One of the key things I learned from her was that her
father-in-law Samuel had fought in the Union Army
during the Civil War. I hadn't known that *any* of my
ancestors had been in the war, so her revelation opened
up wide new avenues of research for me. As you'll see
throughout the book, I've been lucky enough to find
some key records and trace my family back some two
hundred years. Such remarkable bits of luck don't
happen every day, but when they do, they make all the
dogged hours of research worthwhile.

The vast majority of us, unfortunately, will *never* be
able to add that final important piece—to trace our
ancestors absolutely back to Africa. But the challenge
still exists, the chance you *will* be able to add that final
fragment. And even if you can't, even if you're only
able to go back two or three generations, your search
won't be a failure. The family history you'll construct
will be an important part of your own life and an
invaluable legacy for your children as well.

My own search has barely begun. But along the way,
I've discovered something of great importance—the
magnificent strength of the black family. We've *always*
been concerned about our blood ties and have done
everything we could, often under inhuman circumstances,
to preserve them. And though they tried mightily, even

the whips and chains of slavery couldn't destroy us.

Black genealogy is the ultimate puzzle, an adventurous journey through a very personal history. For that reason alone, it's probably infinitely more rewarding if you decide to "do it yourself." Each piece of the puzzle, insignificant by itself, takes on added meaning as part of the emerging whole. The "parts," in this case, are the genealogical chart you're going to learn to construct, tracing your family from your father and mother, through *their* fathers and mothers and so on, as far back into history as you can go. But the sum of your search can be far greater than the parts alone.

If the search makes you prouder to be black, prouder to be *you*, then it's been successful. Finding out where you came from just might make it easier to figure out where you're going. You'll be joining a growing legion of blacks all trying to do the same thing—regain some pride in a history that so many people have tried to make us forget or be ashamed of.

Chapter Two

WHERE TO BEGIN

Figure 1.
BASIC FAMILY TREE

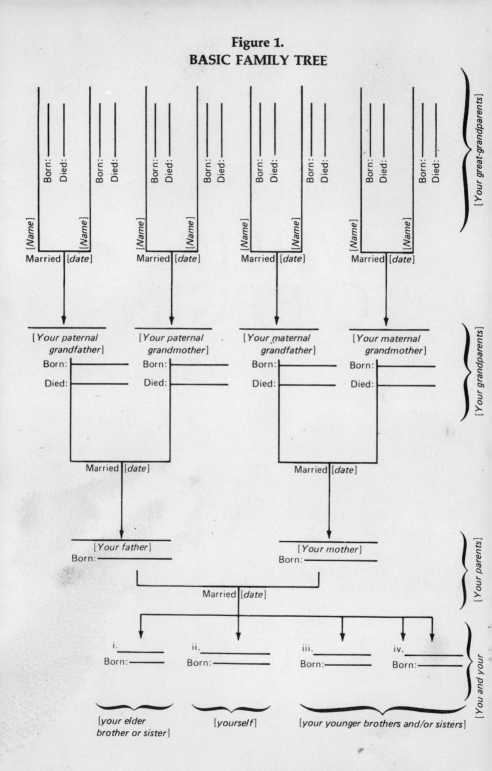

The Family Tree, the one obvious symbol of genealogy that looks so perfectly framed on the wall, is really a summary of your findings. Figure 1 shows a typical blank tree with spaces for the last four generations of your family. The most recent generation—you, your brothers and sisters—is at the very bottom. The higher you go on the tree, the farther back into time you travel and the more the tree begins to "branch out." This is why we so often speak of "descending from" a given ancestor—in this kind of chart, the offspring are always on the bottom.

Because such a tree is only a summary, the only information included on each relative is name, dates of birth, marriage, and death. Logically, you should begin with what you already know about yourself and your immediate family. Start at the bottom and fill in this information for yourself and your brothers and sisters. Then go up to the second generation line, filling in the information for your mother and father.

How did you learn this information? By asking them, of course! And it should please you to know that by doing so, you're reviving one of the oldest black traditions of black culture—the so-called oral history. In Africa, each family had a *griot* or archivist who committed the family's entire history to memory. Each *griot*, in preparation for death, would hand over his entire log of historical stories to a younger man, who became the new family historian. In this way, a family could always trace its history back hundreds of years.

Just by completing this first phase of the chart, you can see how much information you were able to collect easily from immediate family members. That *was* the easy part, since it all relied on what was already family knowledge.

Figure 2.

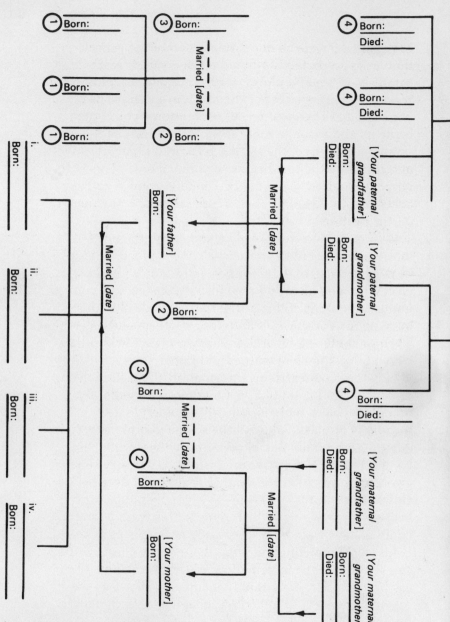

COLLATERAL FAMILY TREE

Circles marked 1 represent your cousins. Circles marked 2 represent your mother's and father's brothers and sisters—your uncles and aunts. Circles marked 3—the people *they* marry—are your aunts and uncles by marriage. Circles marked 4 represent your great-aunts and great-uncles.

You might want to make two separate charts, one showing your direct family line and another, more detailed one that would include aunts, uncles, and other collateral relatives. The first chart will still be your best yardstick of progress into time, but the second chart, while messier, will be more complete. Figure 2 is a sample of a three-generation chart that includes these other relatives, showing how to attach the various lines between them.

In Figure 1, the third line is for your two sets of grandparents, and the fourth (if you can), for your great-grandparents—eight in all. But always remember that chart, the family tree, is little more than a *summary* of your detailed findings. What you're really doing is compiling a family *history* that's as complete as you can make it. After all, simply discovering the names of your ancestors isn't the sole reason for the search; unearthing where and when some great-great-relative lived isn't enough. You want to find out *how* they lived and really get a feel for the world and society they inhabited.

Keep the information for each family member on either separate note cards or pages in a notebook—your main supplies. The file cards or notebook can follow any particular system you feel most comfortable with, but no matter which method you use, use it *consistently* for every bit of information you collect. Your system should contain the following basic information on each person:

1. Name.
2. Date and place of birth.
3. Address (include past addresses and dates he or she lived there).
4. If no longer living, date and place of death.
5. Education, including names, addresses, and dates of attendance for each school.
6. Occupation(s).

7. Places of employment, with addresses and dates.
8. Names and addresses of parents.
9. Marital history—if married, when and to whom.
10. Changes of name—for whatever reason, including marriage. Always include *all* of the names and their various spellings.
11. Names and addresses of all children. Number each child with a Roman numeral (i, ii, iii, etc.) to identify the order of their birth. If the person sired a number of children with different spouses, always note the child's real father and mother along with any adopted or foster parents.
12. Church, political, club, or society affiliations, including offices held and names of key friends (for further information).
13. Public offices held.
14. Military service record.
15. Honors received—scholarships, grants, awards, medals, etc.

Also remember to record not only the information you collect on each family member, but where, when, and from whom you received those facts. If you run into inconsistencies later—over a birth date, for example —such notes will make it very easy to recheck your data and figure out which source was wrong. Organization is really a key—a good system of record keeping will really pay off in the long run. You'll see for yourself how important this advice is when you start to put the information together, relating the various items one to another in later stages of research.

Despite the family tree's abbreviated character, you can use it as a yardstick for measuring your progress, since it's easy to see where the gaps are. You might be able to fill in part of the fifth generation—your great-great grandparents—but you'll probably have only scanty information on one or two out of the sixteen.

Keeping the oral tradition in mind, you are now ready to begin your own real research. In all of this initial oral research period, interviewing is the key. You started with your mother and father; so now talk to each relative who lives nearby. Gradually work your way to older or less immediate relatives.

If a considerable part of your family still lives in one area, a family reunion on some holiday like Thanksgiving, Christmas, or New Year's offers a splendid opportunity for extensive interviewing. If such an event takes place, be ready to take advantage of the incomparable collection of family history your relatives represent. Familiar keepsakes and heirlooms you have around the house might prove to have unexpected stories behind them.

Never, never, *never* trust your memory with "word of mouth" information! *Write it down immediately and date it*. If you don't make this a strict rule to follow, too many valuable facts will be lost.

As you interview, carefully write down each date, place, and name or relationship they give you. Also note the name and address of the person supplying you with the information. Make such careful note taking a habit. It will help you avoid running back to the same relative to recheck messy or illegible notes.

Taking good clear notes is often not easy, especially when confronted by a great-aunt with a long rich life and a lot of stories to tell. If you know shorthand, it shouldn't be difficult to take down almost the whole conversation. A tape recorder is the easiest method to ensure perfect accuracy, of course, but especially with older people, the sight of a tape recorder might just cause your source to "clam up" entirely. If you can't take shorthand or use a tape recorder, just take notes as best you can.

Make your questions as clear and concise as possible. And be tactful—you never know what hidden family skeletons an innocent question may unaccountably rattle. If necessary, ask the subject to repeat a key date or name. Your questions will often trigger a whole flood of memories. If the conversation drifts to topics that appear to be totally valueless, try to steer your storytellers back onto the right path. But don't be rude or offend them. You *need* their help. So be prepared to be a good listener.

Some of these details will be important, others will appear less so. But take down everything. If you are still at the beginning stages of oral research, it'll be impossible for you to tell yet what's important. You'll be surprised how often a seemingly insignificant detail can become a major clue three or four months later. For example, a black high-school student I know recently began interviewing relatives to gather basic information for his family history. His great-grandmother gave him a lot of invaluable clues that would help him later, but kept referring to her husband as "Scipio"—even though *he* knew his great-grandfather's name was George. When he asked her about the name, unfortunately, she started to wander off onto other topics. No one else in the family could help him make sense of this apparent paradox.

But because he had talked to me before undertaking the interview, he made a note of the discrepancy and forgot about it. One year later, while searching through

piles of slave records in the National Archives, he found
his great-grandfather's name—George—and on a hunch,
tried to trace it further back using the Scipio clue. It
turned out that George's first master had named him
Scipio. "George" was the name given him by a later
master. The seemingly senseless ramblings of his old
relative ultimately enabled the student to trace George-
Scipio back to the auction block and the slave ship that
brought him over from Africa!

After you have interviewed every relative within
reach, try to contact some of your other relatives who
are more geographically scattered. When asking them
for particular information, be as brief but precise as
possible.

Of course, as you interview all these relatives, you
are really interested in more than just their memories.
You want to find the *documents* that will help you
substantiate your findings—perhaps give you even more
vital clues about particular ancestors.

THE DOCUMENTARY RECORD

Consider every attic a potential treasure trove of
information. Many black families, for example, recorded
important data in the big family Bible, including dates
and details on births, deaths, weddings, and other
memorable events. Scrapbooks, baby books, and diaries
often contain a wealth of pictures and articles.

Since photography became fairly popular during the
Civil War, you might be lucky enough to find some
pictures or glass negatives of some otherwise obscure
ancestor. When you find old photographs in boxes or
trunks, take the time to write on the backs the names of
the people in the pictures and their relationships to each

other. If you don't know, ask—or when Grandma or Great-Uncle Joe dies, there may be no one left to identify them. Also write down—wherever possible—the *date* the photograph was taken, because a person's appearance can change over the years.

Distant relatives may also turn up with historical gems only you can appreciate. If sent by mail, make sure the package or envelope is certified to avoid loss or delay. If you can afford the trip, visit the relatives who own the documents you want and go through them firsthand. Such visits might turn up still other documents your cousin or great-aunt didn't even think were important enough to tell you about.

While most people will be unable to devote a major portion of their time to this search, even a small effort can at least preserve some of these documents, important historical records that might otherwise be lost forever. For this reason, any piece of information—an old photograph, a mill or sharecropper's record—should be carefully preserved, even if it seems totally insignificant. Eventually, it will probably occupy an important place in your family's history. But be careful to maintain accurate records of your findings. Copy down the dates of the entry or correspondence and the names and addresses of the writer and addressee. Also record where the particular item is—or who owns it—in case you want to return for some additional research.

Whenever possible, try to get copies of these documents. Photocopies—if you can borrow the document for an afternoon—ensure a perfect replica. But when you extract material from old letters or diaries, for example, be sure to make *exact* copies of the original *including* misspellings, even of your family name. In my family Bible, for instance, "Blockson" is spelled three different ways! But as I learned from other sources, the family name was spelled in a number of ways: Blocksim, Blocksom, Blockson, Bloxam, Bloxham, Bloxom.

If you copy down information such as obituary notices from old newspapers, make sure you include the name and date of the paper. Such care will save you from the frustration of going back to some cut-out article and discovering that the all-important date of the event is missing.

From now on, oral history will be only a minor tool in your work. Your next step is into the labyrinth of official records to fill in the gaps in the fourth and fifth generations and attempt the sixth, seventh, and on beyond. You need to begin a long search for written records of all kinds.

Much of the searching through musty courthouses will turn up nothing, but there is no way of knowing ahead of time which specific sources will be valuable. Above all, remember that clues, *any* clues, are now the key. You can never tell where those clues will turn up or what form they will be in. But your further researches will take very specific directions, as I'll explain in the following chapters.

Chapter Three

PUBLIC RECORDS AT YOUR COMMAND

Even though you've only read through two chapters, already you'll have had varying degrees of success. You may have managed to piece together most of five generations; or perhaps you're having trouble just getting through the second or third. But you should have exhausted the memories and attic relics of all your accessible living relatives. If you *haven't*, go back to work with your tape recorder! Otherwise, it's time to hit the records.

This next phase of your research should be just as organized as the first. Before you consider a journey to Louisiana to trace a great-uncle, sit down and evaluate what you have—and what you still need.

NARROWING THE SEARCH

Start with the files on your mother and father. Is there any information you're missing? If so, does your research indicate where to look for it? Put all of your gaps on a separate sheet, a long list of *all* the information you need and where (you think) you can find it. Do the same thing for each generation you've managed to trace even partially. Don't be discouraged if the list of missing data seems uncomfortably long. If you look closely, you'll see that many of the missing facts are dates, places of birth or death, or similar items.

So as to simplify your search, divide your needs into geographical areas. Put the youngest people first. (The *younger* the relative, the easier the facts on him will be to locate. The *older* the relative, the more basic data you'll require and the longer the search.) But in this phase of your work, narrowing the search to a given locale is your most important chore. The more specific your geographical information (e.g., city rather than

state), the less you need to do, since you'll be able to
concentrate on that single location without having to
make numerous other trips to far-flung storage bins.
Once this is accomplished, you're ready to begin finding
some new data.

If you have little love for musty libraries and old
courthouses you might resent the time-consuming,
sometimes boring slog through reams of dusty records
that your search now requires. Or you may be so
satisfied with the results of your oral quizzing that you'll
feel little need for such work. But remember that
genealogy can be a lifelong hobby. There's no reason to
try to do everything in only a week, or lay out a lot of
time and money right away to uncover a single elusive
clue. Don't be too ready to give up so easily. If you
spread your search over period of years, its story will
unfold just as marvelously, if not quite as speedily.
Read the rest of this book for a thorough grounding in
the procedures to follow and *slowly* add to your
knowledge about your family.

Always start with the easiest task first—relatives
missing only some vital statistic, such as date and place
of birth, death, or marriage. The longer your family has
remained in one geographical area, the easier it'll be to
fill in your history.

The Bustill family has lived for many years in
Philadelphia. The patriarch of the family was Cyrus
Bustill, born in Burlington, New Jersey, on February 2,
1732. After learning the baking trade from a Quaker, he
went into business for himself. His bakery prospered,
and he donated large sums to promote the cause of
freedom. He and his Delaware Indian wife, Elizabeth
Morey, had eight children. During the Revolutionary
War, Bustill supplied the American soldiers with bread.

General George Washington gave him a silver piece as a souvenir; one of the members of the Bustill family still has this treasure today.

After the war, the Bustills moved to Philadelphia and became Quakers. Cyrus opened a bakery at 56 Arch Street, where he did a thriving business with some of the leading families of the town. He was recognized as a leader of his people and was a very active member of the Free African Society founded in 1787. He later relinquished his membership with the Quakers to join the Protestant Episcopal Church of St. Thomas. After he retired from his business, he opened a school and became a schoolmaster. One of Cyrus Bustill's descendants was Paul Robeson, the eminent singer, actor, and humanitarian. Members of the Bustill family are still living in Philadelphia.

The Cardozas of Charleston, South Carolina, a family of black and Jewish descent, can be traced back for almost two hundred years. One member of the black Cardozas was Eslanda Goode Cardoza who became the wife of Paul Robeson. Another distinguished member of this family was Frances Cardoza, who served during Reconstruction in the South Carolina legislature.

A black family of long standing in Virginia was the Jarratt family. Richard Jarratt was born in Pocahontas about 1779 and married Besty Rollins in 1803. In 1820, he owned a house and a lot in Pocahontas valued at $831.25 (on which he paid taxes of $1.80). In 1828 he further added to his small holdings by buying a lot from one David Cary. Jarratt ran a boat from Petersburg to Norfolk and kept a regular account book of his daily cargo. Another indication of his worth is that he had his children educated. In 1814 he paid Joseph Shappard, another free black, $2.50 per month for tutoring his daughters Jane and Ellie.

One of Richard Jarratt's sons, Alexander, was born in
Pocahontas in 1806 and died in 1869. Like his father, he
took to the water, at one time being a steward on a
vessel which ran to New York. Alexander married
Nancy Fuller of Norfolk. John Fuller of Norfolk and his
four sons all went to Liberia about 1855. One son
became a mayor and the others high sheriffs. For a
while Alexander and his family lived in Norfolk, from
which they made frequent trips to New York on both
social and business missions. Alexander and Nancy
Jarratt had twelve children. Their descendants continue
to live in Virginia.

If you're as lucky as the Bustills or Jarratts, count
your blessings! With such a precise idea of the
geographical area where your ancestors lived, such
information is relatively easy to find.

LOCAL SOURCES

Local directories were similar to the federal censuses
discussed later, but covered only a specific town or city
and were usually more complete. Your local library
should have copies of such early directories.

When checking these sources for the surname you're
tracing, see how far back you can go. If a family name
appears in the 1890 directory, for example, does it also
appear in the one for 1889? For 1888? This year-by-year
check will help you verify that person's residence in a
particular area and get some vital information on the
years he or she lived there.

Probably the directories will tell you whether the
person listed was black, but various methods were
employed to denote color. The Aitken directory for
Philadelphia devoted an entire section to black residents.
The Paxton directory used an asterisk to denote such

Fletcher Thomas, jeweller and silver smith
　　130 Chesnut d h 11 S 5th
　　Thomas S, furrier 103 1-2 Christian
　　Thos, machine mr 162 1-2 Christian
　　wid Catharine, cake bak 110 N 7th
　　wid Elizabeth, book folder 224 S 7th
　　widow Rebecca, b h 127 Mulberry
Fleu Charles, printer 26 Charlotte
Flick Andrew, currier 128 N 4th
　　Lewis, 23 baker N 7th
　　Sarah, b h 147 N Front
Flickwir Henry, house carp 24 German
　　Jeremiah, drug and apothy 351 S 2d
　　wid Rebecca, gentw 24 German
Flide Sarah, 382 S 2d
Flin Thomas, Boyle's al Passyunk road
Fling Bennet, shopkeeper 22 N 6th
　　Hannah, shopkeeper Davis' ct
　　Susan, boarding house 10 N 6th
　　William B cab maker Harmony ct d h
　　95 Walnut
Flinn Alexander, cordwainer 465 S Front
　　Patrick, laborer Rose al n Green
　　Robert, plasterer 4th bel Master
　　Thomas, mariner 12 little Water
Flint Achilles, cab maker 100 Lombard d h
　　139 S 5th
　　Almond, house carp Green n 3d
　　Erastus, cab mr 10 College avenue d h
　　18 Plum
　　James, machinist Beach n Manderson
Flintham wid Elizabeth, gentlw N s of Wood
　　bel Ridge road & 10th
Flinton Francis, 300 S 3d
Flomerfelt George, broker 58 Cedar, d h 121
　　Swanson
Florence James, shipwright 16 Parhams al
　　and Sheetz, boat builders 30 Swanson
　　Sarah, 111 Queen
　　widow, 11 n Spruce W
Florin John, mariner S E c 4th and Queen
Flowers George, haydealer N 8th 1 door bel
　　Sassafras
Floyd James, weaver Perry bel Pine
　　John, jr gro S E cor 4th and German
　　John, 265 S 3d
Fobes George W, mer 185 High d h Sassafras
　　n 11th
　　William, weaver Centre square W
Fœring Abra'm P, measurer of grain 109 Vine
Fœring Frederick, jr dry good store 164 N 2d
　　Frederick, currier 6 n Germantown r
　　Samuel, collector of taxes 109 Vine
Fogg Aaron, bricklayer N 12th n Arch
　　Samuel, bricklayer 58 Vine
　　Samuel, gardner Passyunk r n 6th
Fogle Jacob, brick mr Race n Sch 5th
Folbarcht Martin, baker 98 Vine
Foley David, saddler 4 Howards ct
　　John, baker 390 S 2d
Folk John B, mer 9 S Front

Folkrood Elizabeth, shop 296 Vine
　　Joseph, carpenter 174 N 13t
　　Joshua, tinman 42 Juliana
　　Miss, mantua mr 97 Browne
Follanshee John, ladies shoemaker &
　　shop 24 Lombard 58 Qu
Follock Frederick, butcher carpenter
Folwell Charles S, gent 90 N Front
　　Courtland F, tailor 12 N 3d
　　Job and co, shoemaker 312 N
　　Joseph, turner 438 N 4th
　　R F, d h city hotel
　　Thomas & co, merch tailors 2
　　T J & R, hosiers 7 N Front
・　Wm, dry gd mer 9 N Ft d h 23
　　William, jr dry good mer 73
　　h 22 Mulberry
　　Wm & Son, mer 9 N Front
　　Wm, cordw Pitt b Beaver a
　　ders ct
Fonier William, tobacconist 127 Brow
Fontagne Joseph, teacher 4 Castle
　　P F, Walnut ab 9th
Fontaine Fras, sea capt Queen bel Ca
Fontanell Rose, cab & venetian blind
　　157 N 3d
Foote Benjamin E, 29 Dock
　　John, cordw 27 Mead al
　　Nisan, comb maker Broad bel
　　and Stoever, liquor store 29 D
　　widow, innkeep Callowhill be
Forbes Jared, cordwainer 360 S Fron
　　Thomas, cordw rear 105 Cat
　　Wm, weaver Olive n Broad
Force John, cordwainer 45 Moyamen
　　Rev Manning N 4th front of the s
　　Miss, 75 Mulberry
　　Peter, cordwainer 275 S 4th
　　Richard, cordwainer rear 159 C
　　Richard, cordw 406 N 4th
Ford Augustus, carpenter 114 Cherry
　　Charles, Sassafras near Sch 8th
　　E, milliner 75 Mulberry
　　George, carpenter 103 N 7th
　　J, merch 206 High
　　†Jacob, waiter 199 Shippen
　　Jesse, house carpenter Wood ab
　　John M, plated saddlery 32 N
　　†John, hair dresser 109 Pine
　　Thomas, cotton manuf 36 Palm
　　Wm, manuf plated saddlery 7 N
　　135 Vine
　　wid Ann, grocer 337 S Front
Forde George, house carp 6 Nichols
　　Gustavus, 10th near Sassafras
　　John, mer 8 N 7th
　　Mary, shop N W c Sch 3th &
　　William, baker 92 Cherry
　　widow Elizabeth, 7 Hoffmans
　　widow Jane, mantua mr 211 S
　　wid Mary, seamstress 16 Wag

Figure 3.

In this Philadelphia City Directory for 1811, a cross is used to denote "persons of color." Early directories like this are usually housed in

wid Sarah, dry good store 86 Mulberry
widow, shopkeeper High near Schuyl
permanent bridge
and Samuel, printer South ab 10th
augh Solomon, tobacconist 64 Race
Wm, currier 42 N 7th d h 261 N 3d
wid Christianna, washwoman 12
Kunckle
wid Mary, drygood sto 261 N 3d
Catharine, grocer Prosperous al
Edward, stone cutter 13th bet Cherry
& Mulberry
Edwin, tragedian 144 N 10th
George, cordw 114 Frankford road
widow Rebecca, 10th n Vine
n Isaac, labourer 81 N Juniper
Isaac, gentleman 13 Wood
John, machine mr 262 S Front
John J, cordw 2 Drinkers al
William, shopkeeper 291 S 7th
a John, teller in N L bk 47 Old York r
t John, butcher 87 N Juniper
ter Peter, clothier 248 S 6th
widow Catharine, b h 63 Chesnut
(See Fourester)
Abraham, victualler 62 Garden
Fredk, upholsterer 16 Raspberry al
William, weaver Walnut W of Sch 8th
h J, Lombard E of Sch 8th
James, stone mason 225 Shippen
Thomas, carpenter 168 Coates
wid Elizabeth, gentw 194 Pine
aniel, bricklayer Cherry n 8th
evi, cordwainer 13 Gaskill
ouis, accountant 168 Spruce
John, barber 384 S 2d
n James, sail mr 95 S whs d h 92 Lomb
ue Thomas, house carp 148 Christian
wid, Vine ab 10th
Lewis, shoemaker 58 Queen
r & Gorgas, wood cor Oak n Browne
Ichabod, d h 8 Emlins ct
ok widow Mary, washerwn 12 Juniper
t A, porter Lombard bel 10th
Francis, labourer 163 Coates
Robert, labourer Mark lane
Gab B, cordw St John ab Poplar lane
James, labourer rear 72 Christian
John, caulker Hanover ab Queen
John, tobacconist 155 Coates
Joseph, boot maker 27 Carters al
M, blacksmith 218 N 5th
Mary, gentw 87 Shippen
Matthew S, surgeon instrument mr N
E cor Sansom and 9th
N C, 19 S 7th
Silas, sea capt 36 Almond
r, ladies shoemaker 45 Pine

Foster Wm, cordw 231 Shippen
Wm, mer 85 N Front d h 111 Mulberry
Wm, sea capt 76 Spruce
widow, shopkeeper 26 Tammany
wid Lydia, nurse 11 Passyunk road
Fotterill S G and Brothers, mers 119 1-2 S Ft
Fougeray George J, stove manuf 111 N 2d
H A, stove manuf 189 N 2d
Rene J, stove manuf 99 N 2d
Foulke Charles, gentleman 49 Sansom
H, commis merch 19 Minor
Hannah, gentw 35 Filbert
Misses, 9 N 11th
Richard P, groc 260 High d h 24 S 8th
Sarah, teacher 35 Sansom cor 8th
Wm, com mer 19 Minor d h 9 N 11th
W and H, commis mer 19 Minor
Fouquet wid Mary, gentw Mulberry n Sch 2d
Fourester Ely, mahogany yard Fetter lane d
h 12 N 3d
Fouse Ezekiel, academy 36 Vine
Matthias, shoemaker 271 N Front
Foust George, stone cutter rear 170 N 8th
Henry, saddler Vine bel 13th
Michael, watchman N Broad bel Vine
Fowe Wm, butcher Shackamaxon n Queen
Fowle Henry, butcher 45 Fitzwater
Jonathan, jr atty at law 27 Branch; of-
fice 275 N 2d
Nathaniel, hatter 122 High d h 231
Vine
W Edward, Sicilian consul 411 N 8th
Fowler Charles, blacksmith 132 N Juniper
George, printer Hunter's ct
Matthias, victualler 412 N 4th
Samuel, tobacconist 341 N 2d d h N
3d n Poplar la
Stacy, gunsmith Poplar la n St John's
d h St John's ab Poplar la
wid Rebecca, nurse 68 Catharine
Fox Ann, store 308 S 7th
B K, engraver 367 Mulberry
and Bowers, brick yard South ab Broad
Charles, cordwainer 145 Walnut
Christian, weaver 113 Green
Esther, 367 Mulberry
Evans, carpenter 202 Green
George, printer Sch 8th first bel Vine
George, attorney at law 12 S 7th
Geo, waterman Frankford rd n Bedford
Hiram, sea capt 281 S Front
James, Jones' al near Front
James, upholsterer 29 Prune
Jesse, 14 Jones' al
John P, tobacconist 12 Rachel
John, cabinet mkr 103 Budd
John, victualler 54 Browne

"persons of color"—a more typical approach, especially in northern cities. Such segregated practices were largely discontinued after the Civil War, and blacks were then listed among the general population.

Cemetery Inscriptions: In addition to birth and death dates, tombstone epitaphs often provide information on occupation, cause of death, marriage dates, names of wives and children, and fascinating verse. The following example was taken from the grave of Amos Fortune, who purchased his freedom in 1770, when he was sixty years old, and began a tannery business in Jaffrey, New Hampshire, ten years later. When he died, he was a highly respected citizen. He left his small fortune to the Quaker Meeting and school district in his community. Each summer he is commemorated at the meeting he attended. Many slaves who strove for respectability by determination, courage, and exceptionally hard work died forgotten, but on Amos Fortune's headstone in the Old Burying Ground in Jaffrey, one can still read:

Sacred to the memory of Amos Fortune, who
was born free in Africa, a slave in America,
he purchased liberty, professed Christianity,
lived reputably, and died hopefully.

Another example of such biographical tombstones is in a black cemetery in Concord, New Hampshire, where twelve hundred former slaves are buried:

God wills us Free, Man wills us Slaves
I will as God wills Gods will be done
Here lies the body of John Jack
A native of Africa who died
March 1773 aged about 60 years
Tho' born in a land of slavery

He was born free
Tho' he lived in a land of liberty
He lived a slave
Till by his honest, tho' stolen labors
Which gave him his freedom
Tho' not long before
Death the grand tyrant
Gave him his final emancipation
And set him on a footing with kings,
Tho' a slave to vice
He practiced these virtues
Without which kings were but slaves.

Birth and death certificates are usually found in the area where the events took place. The files are kept in the vital statistics offices of the state, county, or city; and certified copies can be obtained for a small fee. In the Appendix, I have included a state-by-state listing of vital statistics offices along with complete addresses and dates for which records are kept. Letters requesting copies of any of these documents should include as much of the following information as you already have:

1. Full name.
2. Sex.
3. Race.
4. Month, day, and year of the event.
5. Place of the event.
6. Purpose for which the document is needed (You can just say "genealogical research").
7. Your relationship to the person.

But sometimes these documents are *not* filed with the vital statistics offices. If that is the case, you have to try a more roundabout method. If you know the hospital where the person was born, for example, you can write to them for a birth record. (You can even ask if the physician's original records are available.)

If you've traced your family to one particular area, the county courthouse will probably become a familiar hangout—assuming it's anywhere near your own home. Literally truckloads of information can be found here if you know the offices to check out:

Orphan's Court. All adoption records are kept in this particular court, usually in the county seat where the adoption occurred. Unfortunately, it's often very difficult to obtain any information from the clerks because of laws protecting such confidential records. (You'll run into similar problems if you contact adoption agencies; although some have liberalized their disclosure policies in recent years, many still refuse to release any records to researchers.)

County and Court Clerk. His records cover a huge area, including information on elections, bond and tax records, game, fish, dealers, and professional licenses, school appointments and accounts, social welfare cases (especially children and the insane or indigent), jury duty, county property management, animals, livestock, and agriculture. If any relative did any business with the county—such as applying for licenses or permits—the records of it will probably be here.

Recorder of Deeds. A deed is usually in the name of both husband and wife. Any transfer of land or property by sale or will is recorded by this office, although sometimes this information is excluded and can be found only in the minutes of the county court.

Examine how the grantor of the deed came to own the land in the first place—did he buy it or inherit from some other relative? You'll be especially lucky if you find a *multiple-grantor deed*, filed when a deceased's children sell his property. On such a document are recorded the names of the sons, usually listed in order of birth, the names of the daughters, and the names of their husbands. The residence of each person, even his previous addresses, may be listed.

Assessor. This office should also be contacted if your ancestors owned any real estate. Tax assessment records on the property will probably be available.

Circuit Court and Clerk. Records of divorce, naturalization proceedings, back tax suits, firearm and some other permits, and any number of various criminal trials.

Probate Court. All the information relating to wills, including the records of executors, administrators, guardians and curators, property inventories and appraisals and inheritance tax receipts.

These are probably the major governmental subdivisions you would contact, although a particularly difficult search might lead you to officials like the public administrator, justice of the peace (for marriage records), coroner, sheriff (for any ancestor who was arrested but not brought to trial), treasurer, superintendant of schools, or surveyor. But generally such minor officials will have to be contacted only occasionally and only *after* you've exhausted your major sources at the courthouse.

If you write to the courthouse for records, you must often pay a small sum for the search. Request a bill, along with photostatic copy of *all* names beginning with the same letter as the one you're researching. For example, if you're tracing the Smith family, get a copy

of all of the names under "S" in their master index.
Request the S portion of the indexes of wills, taxes, and
any other records that might be helpful.

By getting such index copies, you can make sure all of
the possible spellings of the names you're researching
are covered. If you only got a copy of the page
containing S-M-I-T-H, you'd easily miss important
information on relatives who used S-M-I-T-H-E,
S-M-Y-T-H or some other variation.

There are *two* indexes for land records—a grantor
and a grantee; copies of the relevant portion of each will
be helpful. Find out how regularly each set of records
was indexed so you can request copies of the particular
years you need.

When you receive your copies and find the information
you need, jot down the various records' whereabouts.
For example, if you find a name in the will index, make
a note of the book and page number where the will can
be found. Then provide this information when you
write to the clerk for a photostatic copy of the will.
Such care will make his job easier and probably speed
up delivery. It's also a good idea to avoid requesting a
long list of records at one time. Clerks are human, too,
and tend to put off long, complex research jobs in favor
of simpler requests.

In some cases, you might want to undertake the
search in person. If you do visit a courthouse on such a
mission, don't expect the clerks to run to your aid. Once
they find out you're a genealogist and begin to think
about all those old records you're sure to want, they'll
tend to give you the cold shoulder. But be as courteous
as possible—you'll probably be spending quite a few
hours there. And the clerks will soften eventually; you'll

even find some who love poring through old records themselves!

The ledgers you'll be using will probably be heavy, hard-to-locate, their ink slightly faded and the bindings weak, but any one of them *could* be your personal gold mine. Of course, they might not contain all the information you need. Though the clerks will be loathe to admit it, the really old and rarely used records are often just loose papers stacked in some basement boxes. A friendly clerk might allow you to see them if you ask nicely enough. Don't let a little dust stand in your way!

Many institutions once indicated race on their file cards and other records. The letter *N* indicated Negroes, the letter *W* represented Whites. Most have now eliminated this practice, but you can still be helped by this old custom, as I was when I traced some of my own information.

County historians sometimes keep records in their own files which are not in the courthouse. It might be profitable to contact the historian in his office or at his home, if he works from there. If he has old records, the courthouse may give you some of them, provided they pertain to your family and are recorded in the courthouse ledgers.

Once you have added the information from such records to your files, you are ready to investigate a large variety of other sources for clues about your earlier ancestors. There's no rule for which of these should be checked first—to choose a likely path, you have to use your own instincts and the hints built into your growing history. These sources are basic to your research and don't pertain only to nonslave ancestors, especially since so many of your ancestors were both slave *and* free (and sometimes slave again) during their lifetimes.

Although I've included an extensive bibliography, two books are so important that they can be used as key tools throughout your study. The *Directory of Afro-American Resources* (edited by Walter Schatz, published by R. W. Bowker in 1970) can be used as a supplement to the appendix I've already provided. It lists over 2,000 American institutions—libraries, public and private agencies, civil rights organizations, etc.—and includes the full name, address, and telephone number, a list of publications and full description of the collection for each. If you're running into some trouble just getting started, the directory will point you to some institutions that can help you out.

The second work which could also speed up your research is called *Blacks in Selected Newspapers, Censuses and Other Sources: An Index to Names and Subjects* (compiled by James de T. Abajian, published by Boston's G. K. Hall Company in 1977). This volume is a comprehensive guide to black names and activities and the nineteenth and early twentieth century published sources in which they can be found. It cites references to thousands of individuals culled from black newspapers and periodicals, national and some state census records (especially the western states), city directories prior to 1880, and hundreds of books and pamphlets. If you can find a relative's name here, you've lucked onto a clear research pathway through all of the indexed sources. It could save weeks of efforts on your own, but let's investigate these resources one by one.

The Black Church. If your initial research through court records and libraries hasn't yielded too many significant clues, the schools, churches, or any other organizations the person attended or belonged to might also have such information still on file.

The church has always been the focal point of black family life and has played a crucial role in black society throughout our history. Within the church, benevolent societies, literary societies, social clubs, schools, and other groups were the lifeblood of the family. Church records, therefore, reflect the religious, social, economic, moral, and educational life of the black community. Besides information on marriages, baptisms, and burials, church files often contain the letter that transferred members to another congregation. Such letters could be vital for tracing unusually mobile ancestors.

Some churches, black and white, managed to keep and preserve excellent records from their inception right up to the present. The African Methodist, Baptist, and Catholic churches (especially their Louisiana parishes) fall into this category, although the exceptional records of the Quakers are probably the best.

Early blacks who identified with the Moravians were purchased by them, freed, given jobs, and were buried side by side with white Moravians. The Falashas, or Moorish-Americans, are another good source; they kept records and have a long history in this country.

A Philadelphia landmark is historic Christ Church, rightly famous for the makeup of its early congregations. Seven signers of the Declaration of Independence worshipped there. George Washington had a pew in the church, and Benjamin Franklin is buried in its cemetery. And a number of blacks, free and slave, were members as well. The baptismal and marriage records of this church still exist. For example:

Free Blacks Listed in Christ Church's
Baptismal Record, 1717–1760

June 16, 1717	Jane, a free black, aged 40 years and her daughter Jane, aged 3 weeks
August 13, 1748	Sussee Frame, a free black adult
August 24, 1748	Rose Watkins, a free black woman
June 22, 1752	Dinah—wife of Richard, a free black and son John
July 26, 1752	Ambo—adult female
July 26, 1752	Amy—adult female and her infant son Anthony
November, 1753	Sarah—mulatto—adult female
November, 1755	Emanuel Woodbe and his wife and their daughters Mary Ann and Dianna
March 3, 1756	Hester, daughter of John and Margaret Lincoln, free blacks
June, 1757	Phillis, daughter of William and Mary Derrom, free blacks
June, 1757	Sarah, daughter of John and Tenah Moore, free blacks
June, 1758	Mintis Ginnings, male adult
February, 1759	John, son of John and Tenah Moore (above)
March, 1759	Mary Lambert, adult female
April, 1760	Rachel, infant daughter of Coffee and Letitia Commings, free blacks

As this list makes clear, parishioners were not always baptized right after birth—as is the custom today—but when they *joined* the congregation and were found to have missed baptism in infancy. So be sure to check the dates throughout your ancestors' probable lifetimes. Marriage records, though, establish the exact date important for your family tree—as well as the likely dates of the first subsequent offspring.

Marriage Records at Christ Church

September 27, 1728	Francis and Violetta Bone were married
March 3, 1745	Jacob Simons and Tinea Smith, free blacks
December 27, 1745	Titus and Ruth, slaves of George Emlyn
October 1, 1748	Quako and Hannah, slaves of Mr. Allen Sturgeon
August 10, 1755	Archibald Hector and Violet
June 1, 1757	John Moore, a free black and Philis Arthur
October 2, 1757	William Keen and Cornelia Ray, a free black
March 15, 1766	Thomas Augustus and Beneta —black slaves
June 21, 1766	Jack, black slave of Downe York, and Mary
March 21, 1767	Richmond, black slave of Mrs. Dunlap and Sarah, slave of Mr. Harris
September 30, 1767	Audjo, black slave of Margt. McLauyhlin and Rose, A. Mason's slave
December 31, 1767	Polydore, black slave of Mrs. Allabz and Phyllis, a slave of Mrs. McMurtrie
July 25, 1768	John Fry and Margaret Swelley, free blacks

March 1, 1769	Caesar and Phillis, blacks belonging to Capt. Jenking
May 1, 1769	Richard Croomes and Hagar Johnson, black slaves of free black Joseph Graisbury

Unfortunately, many churches have not recognized the value such records hold for historians and researchers and have simply neglected them. But the records you need might have been donated to a university or historical society to ensure their preservation. Before you give up entirely, ask the pastor if such a transfer of documents has occurred. Moreover, what often appears to be total disaster might just camouflage some unexpected gems. Philadelphia's Mother Bethel African Methodist Episcopal Church is the oldest organized black church in America. Founded by Richard Allen in 1787, it kept excellent, detailed records. Over the years, unfortunately, thousands of files deteriorated through neglect. Many more were simply misplaced or stolen. Yet Mother Bethel still has a complete run of the *Christian Recorder*, their official organ, which gave information about blacks all over the country from 1856. Copies of these priceless records are now kept on microfilm at the Historical Society of Pennsylvania.

Beneficial Societies. Beneficial societies for blacks began with the Free African Society founded by Richard Allen and Absalom Jones in Philadelphia in 1787. Formed for its members' mutual assistance, the society provided such things as burial insurance and assistance to the sick, the poor, and the aged. Similar societies were later begun in other areas of the country, stimulated by a fervent desire to improve the condition of black people. They often played an important part in preventing pauperism and crime.

Unfortunately, most of these societies' records have been lost, although information for some—primarily those on the east coast—is still available from such organizations such as the Historical Society of Pennsylvania, Boston University, and the Boston and New York Antiquarian Societies. See the Appendix for addresses and telephone numbers.

Some historical societies have researched the information available on these groups; their reports, especially if they were made at the time, can provide a useful index. In 1838, for example, the Pennsylvania Society issued a valuable book called *The Present State and Condition of the Free People of Color*, which includes a complete listing of active societies. Some other states have compiled similar lists and indexes that your local library should have.

If you know that a relative belonged to one of these organizations, browsing through its existing records can provide his residence or occupation. Additionally, a check of the early records of social clubs like the John Brown Society, Odd Fellows, Masons, Eastern Star, and Daughters of Isis might provide additional clues for further avenues of research.

Black Newspapers. Written in a more informal, folksy way than today's, old newspapers can be another possible treasure trove. A number of black newspapers have been published for more than a century; most keep extensive back files that are open to researchers. See the Appendix for a complete listing of existing and out-of-print black newspapers and their addresses.

As a first step, write to the publishers of the newspapers you wish to examine, telling them the reason for your interest and the specific time period you're researching. When going through the back issues, scan the entire paper for clues. Check the obituaries, which contained far more details a century ago than they do today. The society pages can be helpful, announcing births, marriages, and other special celebrations. And legal advertisements contain information on lawsuits in civil and criminal courts, divorce proceedings, estate settlements, and other official matters. For example:

ESTATE OF LEAH BLOCKSOM
Seaford, Sussex County, Delaware
Public Auction
Sat. April 7, 1894
At the Hotel Penington, Seaford

Land-lying and being in *Seaford Hundred,* adjoining the town of Seaford and lying on the street or road running across the land known as *"Pea Liquor"* and beginning at the northwest corner of *Hester Cannon's* lot and on the east side of said road thence with said Cannon's lot to the land of *Jacob Williams'* heirs, thence northward with the Williams land forty feet to the lot of the *"Good Samaritans"* thence with said westwardly to said east side of said road thence southwardly with said road, to place of beginning, together with the two story frame dwelling and other buildings, thereon. Being the real estate late of Leah Blocksom, deceased, and will be sold by her executor pursuant to power and authority given said executor in and by the last will and testament of said deceased.

Henery W Baker
Executor of Leah Blocksom Deed
Dated March 23, 1894

Employment records can sometimes be obtained from a specific factory or business that is still in operation.

In some cases, the local or state historical society can provide access to the books of an early industry. Blacks had nearly as many diverse occupations as whites, but were especially active in such artisan industries as silversmithing, charcoal making, and iron working. The work records of such industries can be helpful in tracing an ancestor. Here is an example of information from the account books from the Hopewell Village Documents in southeastern Pennsylvania (Hopewell, once an iron foundry, is now a protected historic site).

October 1, 1802	Black Frank began work at the furnace
October 15, 1802	Furnace Dr. to Dan strunk for a pair of shoes for Black Frank
November 2, 1802	Cash paid to Black Frank for 15 days work 1—12/2 Left Furnace
June 22, 1803	This Day Black Dine Came
June 27, 1803	Paid cash to Black Dine 7/6
July 14, 1803	This day Black Dine went away
July 29, 1803	Black Dine as made 3 weeks and 2 days @ 6/per week

Prison Records. Some prison records, including those for local jails, have been turned over to their respective state archives. There is no way to tell in advance if the records you need have been preserved, but if you know or suspect that a relative served time, visit the archives and check. The record of the trial should also be available in the court records.

Almshouses. Many larger cities maintained almshouses for the poor and destitute. Though few such records have survived, what has been preserved will probably be included in the city or county archives.

NATIONAL RECORDS

Census Records. All national census records are available at the National Archives. Rather than prepare for a trip to Washington, D.C., however, you should work through one of the Archives' regional branches (listed in the Appendix). The main offices have been so swamped with requests in recent years that they are unable to handle any genealogical questions, but the regional branches provide research rooms, a reference library, microfilm equipment, and document reproduction facilities. You can often start in your local library and then contact the Archives branch when you need specific information.

Census records are not easy to work with. Checking one fact can take all day. The records' organization is the chief drawback. Although all censuses break down their records into counties and townships, the names under these subheads aren't alphabetized. Even the townships and counties aren't always alphabetized. All of these records are being transferred to computer tapes for easy storage and alphabetizing, but indexes haven't been compiled yet. Regional branches, however, will have copies of each index as it appears, so stay on the lookout.

You'll find the national records remarkably complete —only one census year, 1890, is missing, its entire file destroyed by a St. Louis warehouse fire. And some national censuses have already been indexed by brave, individual researchers. Three are especially important for our purposes:

The year 1790 was the date of the first federal census. Happily, a *List of Free Black Heads of Families in the First Census of the United States, 1790* is available from the National Archives. Names are alphabetized under each state; each entry includes the number of people in the family and the applicable page number from the 1790 Census volume.

The original census act stipulated that all free persons should be listed, but there was no specific provision for free blacks—they were simply included in the "other persons" category, which also included American Indians. Free black heads of families were listed, but census takers were not consistent in their methods— some indicated that a family was Negro, mulatto, or free, while others provided no racial designation at all. Information included the number of family members and their ages, but until the 1850 census, only the *heads* of households were designated by name.

Slave schedules were made for every state—a practice that continued, in fact, until 1860. Each state listing was further broken down by county, with slaves listed under their owners' names.

Unfortunately, these earliest census records aren't complete—the records for Delaware, Georgia, Kentucky, New Jersey, Tennessee, and Virginia were destroyed, presumably when Washington was burned by the British during the War of 1812. The files for Delaware and Virginia were reconstructed, however, so the records still contain these two plus eleven other states: Connecticut, Maine, Maryland, Massachusetts, New Hampshire, New York, North Carolina, Pennsylvania, South Carolina, and Vermont.

From *the 1830* census, Carter G. Woodson, a noted black historian and founder of the Association for the

Study of Afro-American Life and History, compiled
information for two books: *Free Negro Heads of
Families in the United States in 1830* and *Free Negro
Owners of Slaves in the United States in 1830*.

Woodson's second title may come as a shock to some
of you—it *is* a rare thing to find any information on
black slaveowners, because the existence of such men
threatened the ruling class's principle of white superiority
on which slavery was maintained. But such black
slaveowners were not entirely unknown. Anthony
Johnson, who arrived in Virginia in 1619 aboard a
vessel that had captured a Dutch ship and its slave
cargo, was probably the first on record. The blacks on
board were all made indentured servants and eventually
given their freedom. Johnson became a wealthy
landowner and slave master.

But despite other similar examples, many free blacks
recorded as slaveowners gained the title on a technicality.
Many of them merely purchased friends or relatives
from white masters; the very act of sale, therefore,
made them slaveowners in a strictly legal sense, though
none of them considered their fellow blacks as property.

I used Dr. Woodson's *Free Negro Heads of Families in
the 1830's* in tracing the Mounteer family of Montgomery
County, Pennsylvania. The first black settlement in
Montgomery County was founded by freed slaves. It
was named Guineatown (based on the word "Guinea,"
a common term for a black person) situated between
Abington and Cheltenham townships. The son of a
French Huguenot named Richard Morrey (or Maury)
freed the slaves who had belonged to his deceased father
in that area.

Of the land that he had inherited, he leased one

hundred acres for five hundred years to Mrs. Mounteer,
who couldn't legally own property because she was
female. Richard Morrey later gave Cremona Morrey—a
slave who took her master's name—198 acres. The land
was deeded to her husband, John Frey, and five other
free blacks and then placed in trust of Isaac Newton of
Abington. The land was again sold after the Revolutionary War and several estates were formed, including the
first home of Thomas Wharton, president of the
Executive Council of Pennsylvania, and Gray Towers,
now part of Beaver College. Guineatown is now known
as North Hills. The name Mounteer is taken from
Morrey. Today the Mounteer family is no longer found
in that area, but it can still be traced in Montgomery
County.

Both of Dr. Woodson's books can be purchased from
the Association for the Study of Afro-American Life
and History, or borrowed from libraries. Most state
libraries have copies; local libraries can obtain them
through interlibrary loan.

(Contrary to common belief, librarians can do more
than simply supply books. They can usually locate
obscure materials and even suggest resources that
you've overlooked. Get in the habit of asking librarians
for help with your research. They'll usually be happy to
oblige.)

1900 Census: During the 1930's the Works Progress
Administration prepared Soundex, a state-by-state index
to the 1900 census, now available on microfilm. Each
state Soundex has been filmed as a separate publication.

Besides the national census records, certain state
censuses—more detailed, sometimes more easy to
locate—will be helpful. For instance, Kentucky was one

Southwark District
Census Department   Occupatio

Name of Family	Residence	Whole number	the Slaves of the State	the not Natives	Of Males	Of Females
Goldsmith Sarah wid	Swanson st 9	3		3		Dau
Mikhel Robert	Parham st 21	4		4	Porter	washe
Brown George	Do	2		2	Baker	
Chase Elizabeth	Do	1		1		Serv
Scott Solomon	Collins al	7	6	1	Lab	wash
Einven Samuel	Do	1		1	too old to work	
Purkins Thomas	Do	8	4	4	Carter	rous Day
Sworden James	Christian st 28	5	3	2	Lab	wor
Price Joseph	So front st & Canal	11	3	8	Ship Carpenter	
Marlove Jacob	Do	5	3	2	Well Diger	Acm
Camblll Aaron	Do	3		3	Porter	Nick
Greffen Peter	Do	4		4	Lab	Do
Laws Zedock	Do	3	2	1	Do	Sic
Burton Moses	Do	5	2	3	Cook	Serv
Lloyd Hannah wid	S 2 st Meads al	3	2	1		wash
Gibson Elizabeth wid	Do	2	1	1		Do
Fielden Robert	Do	3	2	1	Carter	
Haward George	Do	5	5		Porter	was
Brown William C	Do	1		1	Basket make	
Fasley Jeremiah	Do	5	4	1	Carter	was
Haley John	Christian st 70	4	3	1	Lab	
Haward William	Laviess Cort	4	1	3	ocom picker	D
Bagwell Edward	Do	6	4	2	Brick Layer	Star
Green Samuel	Do	1		1	Lab	
Lewis John	Do	2		2	Do	Day
Fletcher Stephen	Do	4	2	2	Seaman	
Bell Stephen	Do	3	1	2	Do	Serv
Greeves Rosanah wid	Do	8	4	4		was
Wilmore James	Do	2		2	Lab	Day
Miller Jacob	Do	3		3	Do	
30		118	52	66		

Figure 4.

Local censuses were sometimes made for tax purposes. Benjamin C. Bacon's handwritten *Census Statistics of the Colored Population of Pennsylvania* lists an unusual amount of information: each family's

Value of property (Real Estate)	Ground Rent	House Rent	State Rent	Amt of tax	Day School		How freed and Cost	Amt paid for freedom	By whom	Sund. school	able to read & write	Name of meeting which you attend
150		26			1					1		Baptist
100		56			1		By self	300	40	1		Bethel
100		100					freeborn				1	B Wesley
20		10					do				1	St Thomas
200	15			1=31	2		do			2	1	B Wesley
	15			1=31			do					
50		52			2		do			2	1	E Wesley
51		36			1	2	do			1	1	E Wesley
151	22=50			2=25	3		do			2	2	Baptist
300	15 –			3=77	1	1	do			1	1	E Wesley
150				2=58			By self	150		1	4	do
50		32			2		By master			2		do
50		24			1		By self	80		1		Bethel
88	15 –			2=88	1		By master			1	2	1st Presbyterian
300	20			5=00	1		do			1	4	do
150	24			4=92	1		freeborn			1		1 do
60		26			1		do			1		B Wesley
150		48			2	1	do			2	2	Presbyterian
1600		30					By self at 333 Bot wife at 500	800				do
70	14			2.39	2	1				2	7	Bethel
200		64			1					1	3	Presbyterian
30		40				1	By will					E Wesley
100				5=31	2		freeborn			2	2	Bethel
50		30					By master					Wesley
25		30					By self	350				do
50		18			1					1	2	Bethel
41		26				1						
20		14			1	3	By master					E Wesley
15		14					By self	150				do
20		21					By master					do
5	4020 166 50	694		3202 20	18			1863	1340	26	34	

residence, value of real estate, rent paid, number of children attending day and secondary schools, the church each individual attends, and even how each became free! (*Courtesy of the Historical Society of Pennsylvania*)

state which took a special census of free blacks.

Military Records. Black men have fought and distinguished themselves in every American war. For those who need to study their records, the National Archives provides a number of helpful reference works. Three are particularly valuable:

1. *List of Black Servicemen Compiled from the War Department Collection of Revolutionary War Records.* A listing of Revolutionary War servicemen known or presumed to have been black, compiled from three sources in the War Department Collection of Revolutionary War Records. Listed alphabetically by name, with reference to the fuller source where more information can be obtained.
2. *The Negro in the Military Service of the United States, 1639–1886* (on microfilm).
3. *Index to Compiled Service Records of Volunteer Union Soldiers Who Served with United States Colored Troops.* A microfilm publication reproducing an alphabetical card index. Each index card gives the name of the soldier, his rank, and the unit in which he served. There are cross references for names that appeared in the records under more than one spelling and for service in more than one unit or organization.

During the Revolutionary War, for example, over five thousand blacks fought in the Continental Army; another thousand fought on the side of the British. Blacks who fought for the British were called the "King of England soldiers" and were usually fighting for their own freedom as well. Many of them eventually escaped to Nova Scotia. And when the British evacuated after the war, 1400 ex-slaves went with them to London,

Halifax, or the West Indies. *The Book of Negroes*, available in the National Archives, includes the names of these British sympathizers.

Even before George Washington officially authorized blacks to fight in the American forces, a number of blacks had successfully joined the army and found freedom. John Glover's Marblehead Regiment was at least half black, but the courage blacks needed to join their countrymen's war for independence can't be over emphasized. Ned Hector, a free black, began his service March 10, 1777. A private in the Third Pennsylvania Artillery, he was a wagon driver in the Battle of Brandywine. A few years before his death in 1834, the Pennsylvania legislature awarded him a veteran's bonus of forty dollars. His obituary lamented the fact that so little notice was given to his war status. However, in Conshohocken, Pennsylvania, Hector Street is named for him.

Recently the Conshohocken Historical Society asked the Pennsylvania Historical and Museum Commission to commemorate Hector's old cabin site. The commission refused, arguing that Hector had not distinguished himself more than the other twelve thousand men who fought the British at Brandywine. But the committee pointed out that, unlike most of the other twelve thousand soldiers, a black was not welcome in the army. In the thick of battle, blacks were on their own. Thus serving at all had to exemplify extraordinary courage. The commission relented.

Many of the payroll records of the Continental Army, the oldest records maintained by the Federal government, are still kept in the National Archives. Although they are primarily used to establish pedigree for those attempting to join a patriotic society, we, of course, can find better uses for them! The records of a society called the Negro Descendants of the American Revolutionary War is also helpful for tracing relatives during this period.

Daughters of the American Revolution. Good nonofficial sources are the publications of the Daughters of the American Revolution, a group which has been active since 1890 in gathering records of Revolutionary War soldiers and their descendants. There are more than 150 DAR lineage books, each containing one thousand lineages. State branches and individual chapters of the DAR also have published information about Revolutionary War soldiers. Many large libraries have copies of the lineage books and other publications of the DAR (including *Daughters of the American Revolution Magazine*, known before 1913 as *American Monthly Magazine*). Information for using their resources may be obtained from DAR national headquarters in Washington, D.C.

Blacks were active in the War of 1812, but by the 1842 war with Mexico, army regulations had been changed to exclude blacks specifically. Congress was also dead set against their participation, except as servants, cooks, or stewards.

By the 1860's, things had changed—186,017 black soldiers served on both sides of the Civil War. Military records for the eleven black regiments who served at Camp William Penn in La Mott, Pennsylvania, have been carefully preserved.

During the Spanish American War, blacks served in the Ninth and Tenth United States Cavalry and other units. Over 350,000 blacks fought in World War I, almost one million in World War II a generation later. Since, blacks have served actively in the Armed Forces

—in Korea, in Vietnam, and all over the globe. All of these records can be found in the War Department archives, the National Archives and/or the Library of Congress. A variety of regimental records of the Adjutant General's office are also available from the National Archives.

Pension Bureau. Records of soldiers who have drawn pensions are in the Pension Bureau at Washington, D.C. The bureau furnishes transcripts of any applications or other forms relating to pensions. While some of these documents contain only meager information, others abound in biographical data. Should you inquire of the bureau, include as much essential information as you can about the soldier, such as dates of birth, marriage, death, and residence at the time of military service. Address inquiries to the Pension Department, Veterans' Administration, Washington, D.C., 20420.

State libraries and archives often have detailed records as well. Although these pertain solely to that state, they often make it easier to find what you need.

Here and in the Appendix I've listed a large variety of sources, some quite general, others almost awesomely detailed. Choose from among these according to your own particular needs. Often you'll have incredible luck with census or military records; if not, the variety of sources I've included in this chapter should still enable you to fill in large gaps in your family history.

You may have to spend weeks to find even a mention of a single relative. Luck can come at any time, though, and from any direction.

For example, biographies and autobiographies of outstanding blacks recap their history, often revealing information useful for black genealogy. For instance, the well-known black abolitionist, Frederick Douglass revealed in his narrative that his mother's maiden name was Bailey and that she was born in Tuckahoe, Maryland. Douglass' real name was Augustus Bailey. Because of his book, members of the Bailey Casson family can trace their roots back to Frederick Douglass and his parents.

Because these histories are so specialized, they are not likely to do you any good. But, if you're in a local library, it wouldn't hurt to check the card catalogue—you might find a book written by an unknown relative.

The gaps in your family tree that still remain will be attributable, in many cases, to slavery. Although some of the general sources we've discussed will help trace some slave ancestors, most details will have to be supplied from the records of bondage—and ultimate freedom.

Chapter Four

"MAN WILLS US SLAVES"

David Hume wrote in 1768 that "the negroes [are] naturally inferior to the whites. There never was a civilized nation of any complexion than white [!], nor even any individual eminent either in action or speculation."

Hegel noted in his *Philosophy of History* that "it is manifest that want of self-control distinguishes the character of the Negroes. This condition is capable of no development or culture, and as we have seen them at this day such have they always been. . . . At this point we leave part of the world; it has no movement or development to exhibit."

The myth that "Africans are simply uncivilized savages anyway" supported "civilized" rationalizations for the African slave trade. John C. Calhoun, one of the most influential political leaders of the early nineteenth century, felt that the black man was inferior and should stand aside while the superior whites got on with the job of developing civilization. But he did allow that he would consider the black race human if he ever found a black who could understand Greek syntax.

In 1906, a Zulu student at Columbia University commented on Calhoun's generous offer: "What might have been the sensation kindled by Greek syntax in the mind of the famous Southerner I have so far been unable to discover," he stated, "but . . . I could show him among black men of pure African blood those who could repeat the Koran from memory in Latin, Greek, Hebrew, Arabic, and Chaldic." And from a runaway slave ad in the *New Orleans Picayune* comes a poignant testimonial to black learning, even under the handicap of slavery:

FIFTY DOLLARS REWARD. — Ran away from the subscriber, about two months ago, a bright mulatto

girl, named Mary, about twenty-five years of age,
almost white, and reddish hair, front teeth out, a
cut on her upper lip; about five feet five inches high;
has a scar on her forehead; she passes for free; talks
French, Italian, Dutch, English, and Spanish.
Upper side of St. Mary's Market. ANDRE GRASSO

I daresay Calhoun, faced with such proof, would
simply have found some other equally irrational test to
keep blacks "in their place."

Such dispassionate appraisals' effect on human beings,
our slave ancestors, was incalculable. As it was, slavery
became one of the most terrifying chapters in our
history.

Some white historians have tried to rationalize
slavery by pointing out that it was practiced by the
Africans themselves, even before the coming of the
white slave ships. True, but slavery in Africa was a
relatively benign institution, when compared to its
American counterpart. (Madame Tinabu of Nigeria was
a slave trader herself until she discovered the hardships
her kinsman suffered in the New World—whereupon
she became one of the first African abolitionists.) And
never before in history had slaves been shipped across
thousands of miles to a wholly different culture.

African slaves often married into the families of their
owners; some—like Jaja of Opobo—even became local
chieftains. But when white factors or traders arrived on
the coast with muskets, gunpowder, cotton cloth, and
other European goods, unscrupulous Arabs and native
chieftains began using almost any excuse to increase
their supply of negotiable slaves. Wars were begun
solely to capture prisoners to be sent by armed caravan
to the coast. Petty offenses or family squabbles were
often enough to deprive men and women of their

liberty. Africans who worshipped Allah sold condemned criminals to whites so as not to stain their hands with blood. But when the white factors' barracoons were short of a full "legitimate" slave cargo to ship out on the next boat, they had no scruples about making their own captures.

In 1789, Gustavus Vassa wrote a narrative called *The Life of Olaudah Equiano or Gustavus Vassa the African.*

> One day, when all our people were gone out to their works as usual, and only I and my dear sister were left to mind the house, two men and a woman got over our walls, and in a moment seized us both and, without giving us time to cry out or make resistance, they stopped our mouths and ran off with us into the nearest wood.

The ties to his African home in Benin were that easy to cut. He was eleven years old. The only family he had left was his sister, and even that comfort would be short-lived:

> When we went to rest the following night, they offered us some victuals, but we refused it. The only comfort we had was in being in one another's arms all that night, and bathing each other with our tears. But alas! We were soon deprived of even the small comfort of weeping together. The next day proved a day of greater sorrow than I had yet experienced; for my sister and I were then separated. . . . It was in vain that we sought them not to part us; she was torn from me, and immediately carried away, while I was left in a state of distraction not to be described. I cried and grieved continually, and for several days did not eat anything but what they forced into my mouth.

As an adult, Vassa could look back and reflect on
those he called "nominal Christians." "Why are parents
to lose their children, brothers their sisters, or husbands
their wives? Surely, this is a new refinement in cruelty,
which, while it has no advantage to atone for it, thus
aggravates distress, and adds fresh horrors even to the
wretchedness of slavery."

Estimates of slaves deported from Africa since 1400
are between *50 and 100 million people*. The conditions
under which the slaves were kept in the ships that plied
the waters between Africa and America were inhuman.
In *Africa and the American Flag* (1854), the author
describes the captured slave ship *Spitfire*:

> Between her decks, where the slaves were packed,
> there was not room enough for a man to sit, unless
> inclining his head forward; their food was half a
> pint of rice per day, with one pint of water. No one
> can imagine the sufferings of slaves on their passage
> across, unless the conveyances in which they are
> taken are examined. A good hearty Negro costs but
> twenty dollars, or thereabouts, and brings from
> three to four hundred dollars in Cuba.

Sharks followed these ships for hundreds of miles in
search of the human flesh that would satisfy their
appetites. They usually ate well—many slaves and
sailors died en route from fevers and disease brought on
by the subhuman conditions. Some slaves committed
suicide and threw themselves overboard to avoid a life
of bondage.

Gustavus Vassa's narrative appeared in 1789, the
same year that George Washington was sworn in as the
first President of the United States. When Washington
took the oath of office, the "wretchedness of slavery"

had already been receiving legal sanction for more than one hundred years and was so much a part of the young nation that the Founding Fathers had been able to proclaim the equality of all men and the legitimacy of slavery in almost the same breath.

The signers of the Declaration of Independence had deleted Jefferson's condemnation of King George III for condoning the slave trade. But while avoiding any direct mention of slaves or slavery, the Constitution still provided it with the props needed to survive and flourish. A significant part of that support was the three-fifths compromise: by stipulating that for census purposes, each slave would be counted as three-fifths of a person, the Constitution sanctioned assumptions of inferiority and supported the rationalizations for denying even token marks of equality.

Washington, of course, was not the first or the last major historical figure to be involved with slavery. By the Civil War, eleven of sixteen Presidents, seventeen of twenty-eight Supreme Court Justices, fourteen of nineteen Attorneys General, twenty-one of thirty-three Speakers of the House of Representatives, and eighty of 134 foreign ministers had been slaveholders.

Charlie Smith, an ex-slave, was 133 years old in 1976! He remembered that sometime in the summer of his twelfth year, as a boy named M'Icha, he was living on the coast of Liberia. He and some friends were lured onto a "gaily decorated" boat. To their dismay, they discovered that the ship was a prison. The slave ship arrived in New Orleans the first week in July, and M'Icha found himself on the auction block. A Texas ranger bought him and changed his name to Charlie Smith.

Sale itself was the most traumatic form of family separation. Peter Randolph, in *Sketches of Slave Life*, describes the haggling of the auction block:

"Here, gentlemen, is a fine girl for sale: how much for her? Gentlemen, she will be a fortune for any one who buys her that wants to raise niggers. Bid up, gentlemen, bid up! Fine girl, very hearty, good health, only seventeen years old; she's worth fifteen hundred dollars to anyone who wants to raise niggers. Here's her mother; she's had nine children; the rest of them are sold. How much, gentlemen? How much? Bid up! Bid up!"

Poor Lucy is sold away from all the loved ones, and goes to receive the worst of insults from her cruel taskmaster. Her poor mother stands by heartbroken, with tears streaming down her face.

The next "article" sold is Harry, a boy of fifteen.

Auctioneer—"Gentlemen, how much for this boy? He is an honest boy, can be trusted with anything you wish; how much for him?"

Harry is sold from his mother, who is waiting for her own turn on the block. She begins to scream out, "O, my child! my *child!*" But the old slaveholder only threatens her, "Ah, my girl! If you do not stop that hollering, I will give you something to holler for." Poor Jenny, the mother, tries to suppress her grief, but all in vain. Harry is gone, and the children cry out, "Good by, Harry; good by!" The brokenhearted mother sobs, "Farewell, my boy; try to meet me in heaven."

But the worse the conditions, the stronger the blacks' longing for a common sense of identity. During transport from Africa to America, even under the most

BY

HEWLETT & BRIGHT.

SALE OF

VALUABLE
SLAVES,

(On account of departure)

The Owner of the following named and valuable Slaves being on the eve of departure for Europe, will cause the same to be offered for sale, at the NEW EXCHANGE corner of St. Louis and Chartres streets, on *Saturday* May 16, at Twelve o'Clock, *viz.*

1. **SARAH**, a mulatress, aged 45 years, a good cook and accustomed to house work in general, is an excellent and faithful nurse for sick persons, and in every respect a first rate character.

2. **DENNIS**, her son, a mulatto, aged 24 years, a first rate cook and steward for a vessel, having been in that capacity for many years on board one of the Mobile packets; is strictly honest, temperate and a first rate subject.

3. **CHOLE**, a mulatress, aged 36 years, she is, without exception, one of the most competent servants in the country, a first rate washer and ironer, does up lace, a good cook, and for a bachelor who wishes a house-keeper she would be invaluable; she is also a good ladies' maid, having travelled to the North in that capacity.

4. **FANNY**, her daughter, a mulatress, aged 16 years, speaks French and English, is a superior hair-dresser, (pupil of Guilliac,) a good seamstress and ladies' maid, is smart, intelligent, and a first rate character.

5. **DANDRIDGE**, a mulatoo, aged 26 years, a first rate dining-room servant, a good painter and rough carpenter, and has but few equals for honesty and sobriety.

6. **NANCY**, his wife, aged about 24 years, a confidential house servant, good seamstress, mantuamaker and tailoress, a good cook, washer and ironer, etc.

7. **MARY ANN**, her child, a creole, aged 7 years, speaks French and English, is smart, active and intelligent.

8. **FANNY or FRANCES**, a mulatress, aged 22 years, is a first rate washer and ironer, good cook and house servant, and has an excellent character.

9. **EMMA**, an orphan, aged 10 or 11 years, speaks French and English, has been in the country 7 years, has been accustomed to waiting on table, sewing etc.; is intelligent and active.

10. **FRANK**, a mulatto, aged about 32 years speaks French and English, is a first rate hostler and coachman, understands perfectly well the management of horses, and is, in every respect, a first rate character, with the exception that he will occasionally drink, though not an habitual drunkard.

☞ All the above named Slaves are acclimated and excellent subjects; they were purchased by their present vendor many years ago, and will, therefore, be severally warranted against all vices and maladies prescribed by law, save and except FRANK, who is fully guaranteed in every other respect but the one above mentioned.

TERMS:—One-half Cash, and the other half in notes at Six months, drawn and endorsed to the satisfaction of the Vendor, with special mortgage on the Slaves until final payment. The Acts of Sale to be passed before WILLIAM BOSWELL, *Notary Public*, at the expense of the Purchaser.

New-Orleans, May 13, 1835.

NEGROES
FOR SALE.

I will sell by Public Auction, on Tuesday of next Court, being the 29th of November, *Eight Valuable Family Servants*, consisting of one Negro Man, a first-rate field hand, one No. 1 Boy, 17 years o' age, a trusty house servant, one excellent Cook, one House-Maid, and one Seamstress. The balance are under 12 years of age. They are sold for no fault, but in consequence of my going to reside North. Also a quantity of Household and Kitchen Furniture, Stable Lot, &c. Terms accommodating, and made known on day of sale.

Jacob August.
P. J. TURNBULL, *Auctioneer.*
Warrenton, October **28**, **1859**.

Printed at the *News* office, Warrenton, North Carolina.

Figures 5 and 6. _____

When a slave owner moved, his slaves were often auctioned off. Public announcements of such sales were quick to point out the reason *why* the blacks were being sold ("on account of departure"), since sale was a well-known punishment for rebellious or uncooperative servants. The descriptions of each slave's appearance, age, and skills are important clues in your research. (*Collection of the author*)

sordid conditions, blacks maintained that sense of history. They sang chants, clanged their chains, and pounded the sides of the ship. They continued traditional forms of ancestor worship.

Music was another way slaves remembered their homeland. Once ashore, drums became an important way to recall that heritage. (Unfortunately, blacks' use of this primitive telephone became such an effective weapon for communicating and planning revolts that it was soon outlawed by the white masters.) In the West Indies and South America, slaves recalled their African roots through calypso. In North America, the spiritual served a similar purpose. Such songs as "Sometimes I Feel Like a Motherless Child (a Long, Long Way from Home)" and "I Told Jesus That It Would Be All Right if He Changed My Name" strengthened the age-old ties with Africa.

The tradition of the *griot* never died, even after enforced transportation to the New World. *Griots* on the plantation still told their stories, recalling religious cults, community life-styles, even information on where and when various family members had been kidnapped. On the plantation, African myths were still passed from generation to generation. Joel Chandler Harris, a white southern writer, captured much of the black tradition in his Uncle Remus tales—animal folklore stories whose simple charm had important lessons on moral values. The stories were taken almost verbatim from the slaves on various plantations he visited.

But slave masters and the legal and judicial machinery that supported them made many attempts to destroy black family life during those long years of slavery. Those who prefer to believe that masters protected slave families are not facing the reality of the slave institution,

which was, first and foremost, a business. Men and
women purchased other human beings *in order to make
a profit*. Even the masters who tried to keep slave
families intact and allow these families to choose their
own new masters did so only as long as it was
economically feasible.

Slaves were not—and could not be—equal. They
were to provide labor and wealth for their masters and
bring prosperity to the land. And if you are not fully
human, your family is extraneous. Indeed, it may
endanger the slave institution by diverting affection and
loyalty from the master. So the ties continued to be cut,
and the roots weakened.

If the auction block was the most dramatic and
overtly horrible form of separation, other devices were
no less destructive. Moses Grandy, a slave who later
purchased his freedom, tells of meeting a gang of slaves
one day and discovering his wife among them. They
would never see each other again.

But physical separation was by no means the only
factor contributing to the breakdown of black family
life. In the eyes of white society, the black family was a
meaningless notion. Marriage wasn't legally binding and
was often treated as a farce by the master who had to
give his approval to the union. Slaves reported jumping
over a broomstick to seal a marriage, being given old
and ludicrous clothing to wear for the occasion, or
simply being told the conditions of the marriage and
what kind of work was expected from each partner.
Many couples who had been subjected to such degrading
"ceremonies" had themselves legally married after
slavery was abolished.

The master's children had records. They knew their
birth dates, could claim scores of relatives, and talk

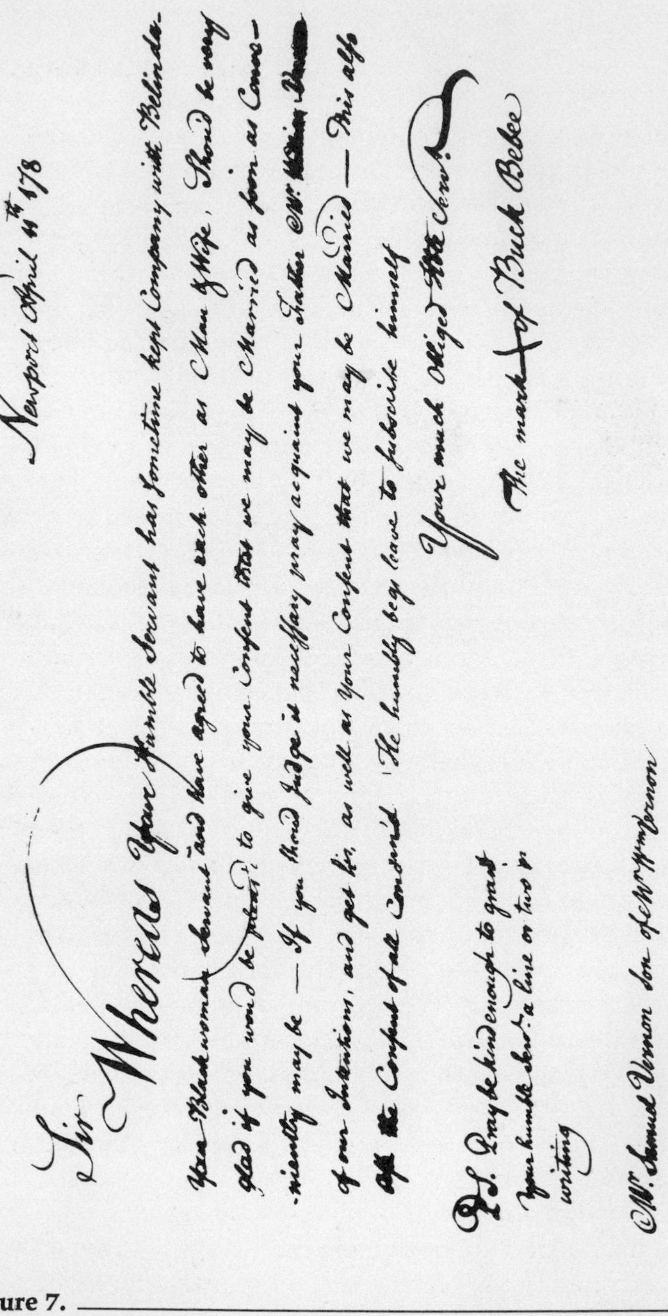

Newport April 4th 178_

Sir Whereas Your Humble Servant has sometime kept Company with Belinda Your Black woman Servant and have agreed to have each other as Man & Wife. Should be very glad if you would be pleased to give your Consent that we may be Married as soon as Conveniently may be — If you should Judge it necessary pray acquaint your father Mr William Vernon of our Intentions, and get his as well as your Consent that we may be Married — His also the Consent of all Concerned He humbly begs leave to felicitate himself

Your much Obliged Humble Servant

The mark of ✕ Buck Bebee

PS. Pray be kind enough to grant your humble about a line or two in writing

To Mr Samuel Vernon son of Mr Wm Vernon

Figure 7. ─────────────────────────

A late eighteenth century slave marriage "certificate" from Newport, Rhode Island. Buck Bebee needed his master's permission ("a line or two of writing") to marry Belinda. But being illiterate, he had to go to a clerk to have his petition written up. (*Collection of the author*)

about grandparents and great-grandparents. But the birth of a slave was not as important as the dropping of a calf. So Frederick Douglass, like hundreds of other slaves, knew only that he was born at planting or harvest time. The year might be remembered *if* it was associated with some particular event. Frederick knew his mother, but seldom saw her. He could only guess his father's identity.

Slave parents were not authority figures in the traditional sense. It was the master's word, not the parents', that dictated their children's behavior. Indeed, a slave father was not even recognized by law. Neither parent could protect his children from the whims of the master or the requirements of the particular plantation. Long working hours usually separated family members during the day and left them exhausted by nightfall. Times of relaxation and sharing were rare. And the ominous knowledge that they could be separated at any time hung over whatever semblance of "family" they'd managed to retain.

Psychological barriers also worked to divide their loyalties. Southern planters often referred to the love they held for their "mammies," black women who served as unpaid nursemaids for white children. Yet such love was always understood in the context of the social environment: a "mammy" was never a social equal. And in adulthood, the planter could no longer even display the affection he may have continued to feel for her. It was worse for the mammy herself, for she often had to devote more affection to the white family than to her own.

White mistresses also had warm feelings for the mammy. After slavery, the same mammy image was transferred to the black woman who was employed in the home and served as a confidante to the entire family. In many cases, primarily in the East, members of wealthy families wrote biographies of their mammies as a way of expressing affection. The affection, however genuine, never crossed the lines of class division, for the mammy, housekeeper, or simply "girl" was never considered a social equal of the white family.

Another divisive factor in black family life was the house slave, whose greater prestige and comfort tended to pit him against the field slaves. Sometimes house servants spied on the master to help the field hands, but they were also known to spy on the master's behalf. Several planned slave rebellions were betrayed by house slaves. After the publication of *Uncle Tom's Cabin* in 1852, the term "Uncle Tom" became popular and was applied by blacks to those who were considered traitors. Perhaps the most intense hatred was reserved for blacks employed as slave "breakers"—blacks who whipped other slaves, sometimes even members of their own families, into submission.

This part of your search could be distressing. It's one thing to read about slavery and see it as an ancient tragedy with little relation to your present life. It's quite another to experience it firsthand through some relative's diary. But despite the pain such a confrontation with slavery can produce, it can also create an unparalleled pride in your heritage. There's certainly no reason to be *ashamed* if some of your relatives were slaves—you should be *proud* they were able to maintain their dignity in the midst of an inhuman system.

Despite the extent and longevity of slavery as an American institution, it's difficult to find equally extensive records. I've included a description of those records that would be most helpful to you and of which some, at least, still exist.

PLANTATION RECORDS

Thousands of detailed records, covering every aspect of plantation operations during the eighteenth and nineteenth centuries, were unavoidably lost or destroyed during the Civil War. Still others were squirreled away in the private vaults of slaveowning families, neglected, or in some cases consciously forgotten. Fortunately, a number of these records managed to survive holocaust and shame, and are just waiting to reveal their secrets to an eager researcher.

Most of these remaining records will be found in the South, usually in the area in which the plantation was located. Most likely they will have been collected in the state archives or in one or two state or university libraries. Check the archives first, then proceed to the libraries. If you're having trouble merely locating a collection, write to the state or one of the local historical societies, which will often be able to point you in the right direction.

Records of former Confederate states—Alabama, Arkansas, Florida, Georgia, Louisiana, Mississippi, North Carolina, South Carolina, Tennessee, Texas, and Virginia—are worth examining independently. Generally speaking, you'll find better slavery records in the northern states, but the South provides many virtually untapped possibilities for genealogical research. Some of these sources require a great deal of time and patience because they are not well organized. You may find no filing system (by name *or* subject) and may have to sift through a great deal of material in search of clues.

To find specific records in a collection of plantation diaries, accounts, and other records, you should know both the name of the slaveowner and the location of the plantation—records can be filed under either. As

Names	Age	Value	Rate	Remarks
Driver Frank	61	—	—	Bedridden and Superannuated
Betty	58	100	1/4	Poultry minder
Carpenter London	42	1.050	Full	Carpenter
Dido	37	650	3/4	
Eloy	17	850	1/2	Small Size
Frank	14	800	1/4	do do
Cleopatra	12	650	1/4	
Evanda	10	500		
Joe	6	350		
Molly	3	150		
Hall George	57	500	3/4	Ordinary Carpenter
Phoebe	32	800	3/4	
George	10	600		
Symphronia	7	300		
Daniel	6	350		
John	3	50		Paralized in left Side
Felix	1/4	100		
Sentee	32	1.000	Full	
Philada	27	850	do	
After	7	400		
Dianna	4	250		
Phoebe	2	150		
Quath	23	1.300	Full	Carpenter, Rough,
Eloy	21	900	do	
Rentee	40	1.200	do	Carpenter good
Jena	36	600	1/2	
Sectind	16	1.000	1/4	
	27.	15.450		

Share A.

Figure 8.

A master's record of his slaves, listing name, value, and occupation. The "rate" means how much work each slave could do—"Full" is the labor of a healthy man. Women and aging men were listed at 3/4, teenagers 1/2 or 1/4. Evidently children under ten were exempt from heavy labor. (*Courtesy of the Historical Society of Pennsylvania*)

usual, the more information you already have, the easier it will be to unearth more. Knowing how many children a particular owner had—or, even better, their names—could help you find records you could otherwise overlook. Knowing the names, you should be able to search *their* records as well as their father's for pertinent information. Since slaves were frequently left to their owners' children, their wills might be a trove of data.

Wills, estate inventories, and tax records prove that slaves were valuable assets to ironmasters in the latter part of the eighteenth century. For example, William Bird of Pennsylvania's Birdsborough Forge lists as part of his property in his 1763 will:

Maria	Wench	42 years old	40
Abagail	Mulatto	22 years old	40
Dick		3½ years old	25
Nedd	Man	35	45
Tom	Man	19	120
Casper	Man	19	120
Tony	Man	26	120
York	Man	65	...
Ebo, subject to fits	Man	35	30
Lembrick		40	45

The slaves could be listed by first name only, or under both names—their last name, of course, might have changed a number of times on the trek from owner to owner.

If no local sources turn up anything helpful, look to the Library of Congress as a last resort. In its collection it has a number of plantation records, family accounts, and diaries of the Old South.

The slave schedules mentioned in Chapter Two might help you locate needed records, too. If you've found the state a given slaveowner lived in, but have been unable to narrow the search to a specific locality, the slave schedules at the National Archives may be able to do this for you. The Archives may also refer you to the pertinent part of the National Census for even more information on the master, his family, and his slaves. Plantation records can also be located in the papers of men prominent in early American life. Among Thomas Jefferson's papers, for example, is the *Farm Book*, which includes lists of his slaves, their parents, and their dates of birth.

SHARECROPPING RECORDS

Many former slaves were sharecroppers, working someone else's land in return for a meager existence and —usually—a state of perpetual debt. While share-cropping records have not always been preserved and are often financially inaccurate, they can at least provide verification of residence. Government offices of the pertinent county should be contacted. The Colored National Labor Union has preserved many sharecropping records for the years 1869 to 1874. These can now be found in the National Archives and Library of Congress.

BREEDING RECORDS

In many parts of the South where slaves were especially scarce, some blacks were used as studs. In some instances, the white breeders deliberately mixed backgrounds in an attempt to produce specific breeds of

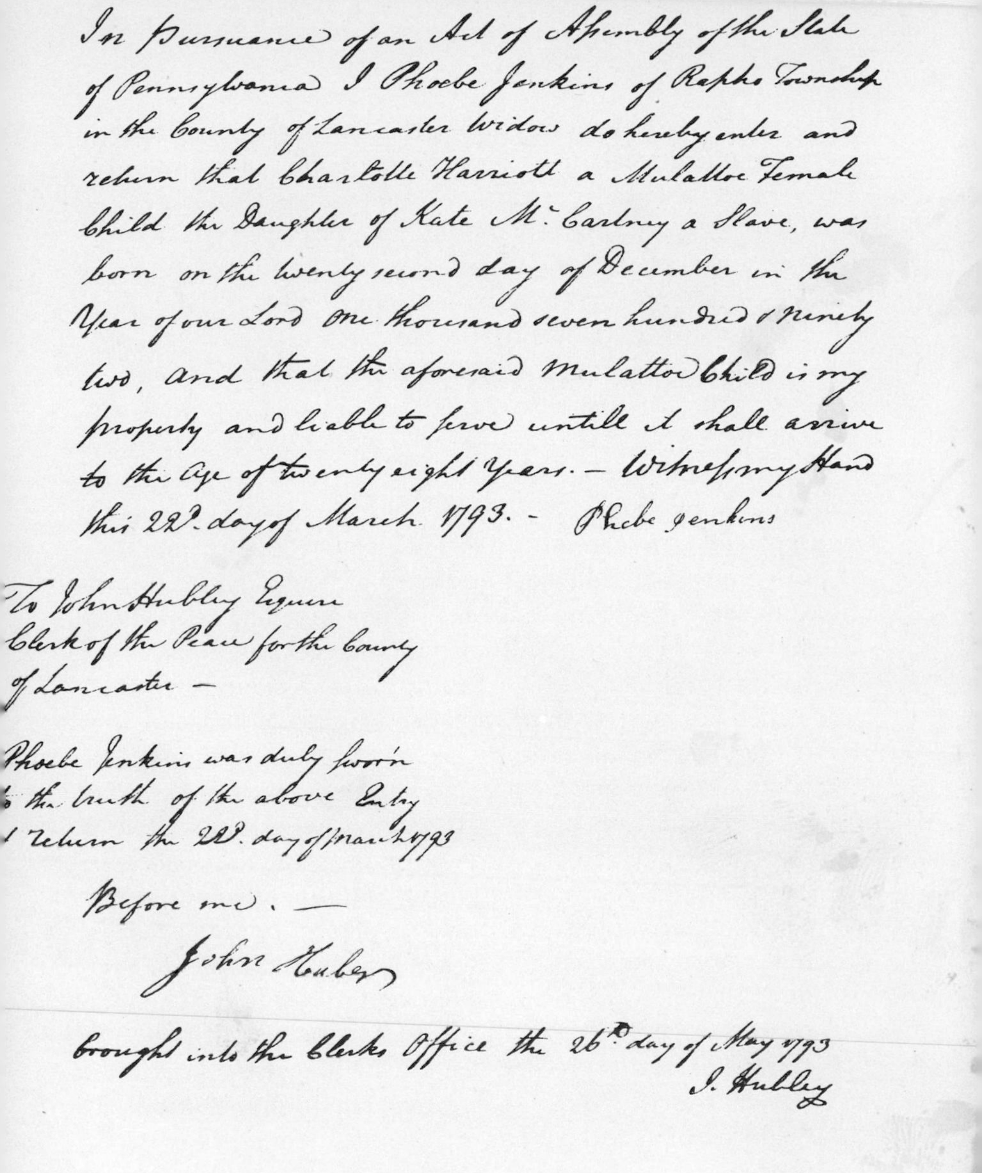

In pursuance of an Act of Assembly of the State of Pennsylvania I Phoebe Jenkins of Rapho Township in the County of Lancaster widow do hereby enter and return that Charlotte Harriott a Mulattoe Female Child the Daughter of Kate McCartney a Slave, was born on the twenty second day of December in the Year of our Lord One thousand seven hundred & Ninety two, and that the aforesaid Mulattoe Child is my property and liable to serve untill it shall arrive to the Age of twenty eight Years. — Witness my Hand this 22d. day of March 1793. — Phebe Jenkins

To John Hubley Esquire
Clerk of the Peace for the County
of Lancaster —

Phoebe Jenkins was duly sworn
to the truth of the above Entry
& return the 22d. day of March 1793

Before me. —

John Huber

brought into the Clerks Office the 26th. day of May 1793
J. Hubley

Figure 9. _____

Slave birth records were sometimes kept to preserve the owners' property interests. Here a widow registers the birth of the daughter of one of her slaves, at the Lancaster County Clerk's office. Charlotte was born on December 22, 1792, after the Pennsylvania Legislature had voted to abolish slavery, so Mrs. Jenkins' ownership was conditional: the child was "liable to serve until it shall arrive to the age of twenty-eight. . . ." (Collection of the author)

slave. It is even rumored that certain plantations were maintained solely for breeding purposes, but no one has yet been able to uncover concrete evidence for such stud factories. After all, few would have bothered to keep permanent records of such a business.

But selective breeding *was* a natural part of plantation life in many areas. Women were given certain incentives to produce children for the master. Some were given their freedom after presenting their owners with a number of offspring. And blacks were not the only studs—white men often took on the "work," fathering children by their own slave women. Emotional ties to such children were virtually nonexistent, for the master often raised them as just another batch of slaves.

In some cases, the records of these breeding sessions still exist. They generally include the ages, national background, and state of health for each slave bred. But sometimes masters even included records of how many children each stud sired by each woman he serviced, what kind of work his parents had performed, and general comments about "attitude" or work value. The term "breeding record" does not refer to any set form. Records were kept in many ways. Breeding was such a source of embarrassment to some plantation owners that records may have been kept in obscure ways, quickly destroyed, or not even kept at all. If such records do exist, they will most likely be part of the general plantation record, but might have been kept in a separate diary. Your search for general information on the plantation will probably uncover them in the process.

Finding other useful sources will depend largely on sweat, sheer luck, or substantial doses of both. It's hard to foresee what clues exist in the unlikeliest places.

SLAVE COLLARS

In the early days of the slave trade, collars were worn pretty routinely to symbolize the slaves' condition of servitude and to control the more unruly ones. Later they were discarded, although masters continued to use them as a form of punishment for slaves who ran away or rebelled in some other manner, a symbol of recalcitrance and troublemaking.

In the true spirit of the institution, slaves even made the collars. They often tried to make them as comfortable as possible, knowing that other slaves, perhaps even a friend or relative, would have to wear them. Generally, they inscribed the name of the master and, later, the name of the slave on the collar. The collars still in existence are in a number of museums throughout the South. The historical society of the state you're researching should be able to lead you to any such collections.

BRANDING RECORDS

In the early years, many slaves were branded as a precautionary method, making total escape virtually impossible. Slaves were most often branded on the coast of Africa before boarding a particular slave ship; the brand usually simply identified that ship. Sometimes, however, the branding occurred at the point of landing. Some slaves bore several brands.

It's difficult to find any records today. Some county courthouses, which recorded such information to discourage runaways, might still have some papers tucked away in a basement. And some institutions retain branding irons as part of their slavery collections.

INSURANCE POLICIES

The Aetna Insurance Company of Hartford, Connecticut, had "Life Department" or life insurance offices in many cities. The New Orleans office, at least, had preprinted forms which slave owners could fill out to protect their property. I've just added two such policies to my own collection: one insures a cargo of blacks being shipped by steamboat from Louisville, Kentucky, to St. Louis, Missouri, in 1856, "ordinary mortality excepted." The other—of which other copies certainly exist—is a printed form with blanks for the names of *individual* slaves. My example insures Maria, a household servant belonging to an owner in Lexington, Kentucky. Though Maria's value is listed at $1,000, the policy is made out for $600 and runs for one year.

LOCAL HISTORIES AND PAMPHLETS

Monograph 31 from the University of Houston, Texas, is just such an obscure source. Called *The Yellow Rose of Texas: The Story of a Song*, it attributes the inspiration for this well-known folksong to a slave girl named Emily. Emily was evidently captured by the Mexican general Santa Ana, who kept her as his "serving girl," more because of her beauty than any talent for kitchen work.

In reality, Emily became far more than just another servant to the notorious Mexican woman chaser. According to legend, Santa Ana himself lost the Battle of San Jacinto because he took an untimely nap. Mexican historians have since concluded that he escaped the battlefield clad in a private's uniform, leaving behind a very confused army of men. When Emily returned to her earlier master, Colonel James Morgan, she told him

about the incident. Morgan in turn related her version
of events to William Bollaert. Bollaert, an English
ethnologist who kept detailed diaries of his trips to
Texas, referred to Emily's story in a July 7, 1842, entry.

Considering the formidable obstacles to facts that the
slave years have erected, you can't overlook even
obscure sources in your search for clues, *any* clues, to
that era. But even if you had success by following the
directions in the first two chapters, you might just find
yourselves stymied in your efforts to trace a particular
slave ancestor.

If you run into uncrackable problems when tracing
your *direct* family line (father to father) through many
slavery experiences, try another tack—trace a lesser
relative, perhaps an aunt or cousin, in the hope that
sooner or later their paths will merge.

But also be ready to live with some unavoidable gaps.
There *are* ancestors who are simply lost in slavery, and
no amount of searching will turn up the necessary
records. And freeing the slaves didn't end the problems
we face, as I'll explain in the next chapter.

Chapter Five

UP
FROM
SLAVERY

The masters had always known what slavery apologists tended to ignore—slaves' best interests would be protected only if they didn't interfere with the master's ultimate sense of power or jeopardize his profits. Not surprisingly, such exceptions were rare. But many masters did free their slaves after a lifetime of enforced service.

MANUMISSION RECORDS

A manumission record is a freedom paper, a formal statement that a slave has been given freedom—or will be given freedom at a specified time. These records appear in different forms; they might be part of a will or a separate document written by the master and given to the slave at the time of his freedom.

Some families still have freedom papers in their possession. Many others are in special collections, primarily those at Northwestern University, University of Virginia, Duke University, Louisiana State University, University of North Carolina, the Pennsylvania Historical Society, the Library Company of Philadelphia, the Schomburg Collection in New York City, Howard University, the National Archives, and the Library of Congress.

The Quakers of Duck Creek Monthly Meeting in Kent County, Delaware, began to keep the Deeds of the Manumission of Slaves in 1743. These records show where and when the slave was born and how long he served as a slave before being freed.

The Pennsylvania Abolition Society, one of the oldest antislavery groups in the country claimed such notables as Benjamin Franklin, John Jay, Dr. Benjamin Rush, Tom Paine, and the Marquis de Lafayette among its

Richard Quest by Will dated thirtieth January 1744 (Inter alia) devises as follows (Item) I will and desire that my Negro Woman named Monemia after my Decease shall be (Free and) Enjoy perfect liberty and not liable to serve as a Slave any Person or persons whatsoever and I do hereby give and bequeath to my said Negro Woman given free as aforesaid One Negro Boy named Polidore (Copy of the said Negro to serve her) and I also give and bequeath (the said Negro Boy) without molestation from any Person or persons whatsoever (to my said Negro Woman) as also to Sum of ten pounds (by my Decease) as also £2 to be paid (by) [...] his heirs [...] one month after my Decease as also [...] to be given her by my Executors of the Negro Boy Polidore given and bequeathed to her as aforesaid within two weeks after my Decease —

True Paragraph

Sam. Williams & [?]

Figure 10. _____

A manumission paper: a slaveowner agrees to bequeath free status to his slave Monemia and her son Polidore, along with an annuity of ten pounds a month. (*Courtesy of the Historical Society of Pennsylvania*)

early members. The society has an excellent collection
of manumission records, most of them on microfilm,
which have been overlooked as a source by many scholars.
In addition, the Genealogical Society of Pennsylvania
has 5,000 indenture and manumission certificates on
microfilm, representing detailed information from nearly
every state on the eastern seaboard plus the British and
French West Indies.

These records are generally filed under certain
obvious category titles (e.g., "Manumission Records of
Virginia"), but can also be found under the specific
master's name. As you've learned in earlier chapters, the
more information you take *in* with you, the more you'll
probably bring *out*. In this case, the master's name and
county of residence *must* be known ahead of time.

ORGANIZED BLACK COMMUNITIES

During slavery, many free blacks owned their own
land and organized communities commonly known as
Guineatowns. ("Guinea" was a term used for a black
person, especially in the north, ostensibly because many
slaves had been taken from Guinea.) Many of these
towns, still in existence today, can be fertile research
areas, especially since a number of freed slaves flocked
to them after the Civil War.

In 1778, four black Revolutionary soldiers founded
New Guinea at Plymouth, Massachusetts. The village
was originally known as Parting Ways. Archaeologists
at this site have unearthed two huge jars believed to
have been brought from West Africa.

In the 1830's Robert Rose and a group of free blacks
founded a small community in northeastern Pennsylvania
known as the Silver Lake Association. Augustus Wattles,
a black man from Cincinnati, founded a settlement in

THIS INDENTURE witnesseth

THAT *Moses* Ganges, by and with the consent of ROBERT PATTERSON and THOMAS HARRISON, members of the Pennsylvania Incorporated Society for Promoting the Abolition of Slavery, he being one of those persons captured on board the Phebe, by the sloop of war the Ganges, commanded by John Maloney, Esq. hath put h——self and by these Presents, the said *Moses* Ganges doth voluntary and of h*is* own free will and accord, put h*im* self Apprentice to *Joseph Malin* *East white land Township chester County — Farmer & Farmer* to learn/h*is*, Art, Trade and Mystery, and after the manner of an Apprentice to serve him the said *Joseph Malin* his Heirs and Assigns from the day of the date hereof, for and during, and to the full end and term of *Nine* years next ensuing. During all which term the said Apprentice h*is* said Master faithfully shall serve, his secrets keep, his lawful commands every where readily obey.

he shall do no damage to h*is* said Master's goods, nor see it to be done by others, without letting or giving notice thereof to h*is* said Master. he shall not waste h*is* said Master's goods, nor lend them unlawfully to any. he shall not commit fornication, nor contract matrimony within the said term. he shall not play at cards, dice, or any other unlawful game, whereby h*is* said Master may have damage. With h*is* own goods nor the goods of others, without licence from h*is* said Master, he shall neither buy nor sell. he shall not absent h*im* self day nor night from h*is* said Master's service without h*is* leave, nor haunt ale-houses, taverns or play-houses; but in all things behave h——self as a faithful apprentice ought to do, during the said term. And the said Master shall us the utmost of h*is* endeavours to teach, or cause to be taught or instructed, the said Apprentice in the trade or Mystery of *a Farmer & Farmer* and procure and provide for h*im* sufficient Meat, Drink, Wearing apparel, Lodging and Washing, fitting for an Apprentice, during the said term of *nine* years *and shall give him three quarters day Schooling*

and when free, to have two suits of apparel, one whereof to be new.

This Indenture not to be assigned, without the consent of the Committee of Guardians of the Pennsylvania Incorporated Society for the Abolition of Slavery.

And whereas a Bond is this day given by *Joseph Malin and Samuel Rickards Junior* to John Hall Esq. Marshal of the United States for the District of Pennsylvania, in the sum of Four Hundred Dollars, conditioned, that if the suits brought or to be brought by the claimants of the Phebe or her cargo: and the Court should determine that *Moses* Ganges is a Slave, then, and in that case, he is (if alive) to be surrendered to the said Marshal or to his assigns on demand.

AND for the true performance of all and singular the covenants and agreements aforesaid, the said parties bind themselves each unto the other firmly by these presents. IN WITNESS whereof, the said parties have interchangeably set their Hands and Seals hereunto. Dated the *eleventh* day of *November* in the year of our LORD one thousand eight hundred

[L. S.]

City of Philad.
Sealed and delivered
in the presence of

Joseph Malin

B. Curran

B. Freeship
Mayor

Figure 11.

A certificate of indenture: when the slaveship *Phebe* was captured in 1800, Moses, one of her slave cargo, was freed by the Pennsylvania Abolition Society and indentured to work as an apprentice in East Whiteland Township. His "Master" was technically his employer in today's sense, though Moses could still be declared a slave if the courts decided in favor of his former owners. All slaves off the *Phebe* were assigned the surname "Ganges" after the sloop that captured her, and the name survives to this day. (*Courtesy of the Pennsylvania Historical Society*)

Mercer County, Ohio, during this same period. Saddlertown, New Jersey, a small community near Haddon Township, was settled in 1837 by a fugitive slave named Jonathan Fischer Saddler. Several residents of this community are direct descendants of this former slave. Perhaps the most prominent of this type of community in New Jersey is Lawnside, which served as a haven for fugitive slaves prior to the Civil War.

The most likely place to find detailed records from these communities are in local and state historical societies, the National Archives, Library of Congress, Howard University, and the Schomburg Collection in New York City.

However vast the power of the slavocracy and its legacy of racism, it could never quench the longing for freedom which is an integral part of the life of a proud people. But plantation owners knew this all too well. And aside from slave collars, branding, and chains, masters used more subtle restraints to prevent slaves from escaping.

Slaves were deliberately kept illiterate—a severe handicap in itself. Some learned to read and write in spite of the prohibition, but it was dangerous to allow one's literacy to be discovered. Mobility was also severely limited—to leave a master's property required a pass. Roads were patrolled, and any white person had the right to stop any black person and submit him to questions. Slaves had no money, of course, and usually little knowledge of the world outside their immediate surroundings. Thus it was extremely difficult for a slave to make any inquiries or contacts outside the local area. To ask a stranger for directions or help was a risk that few dared to take unless desperate.

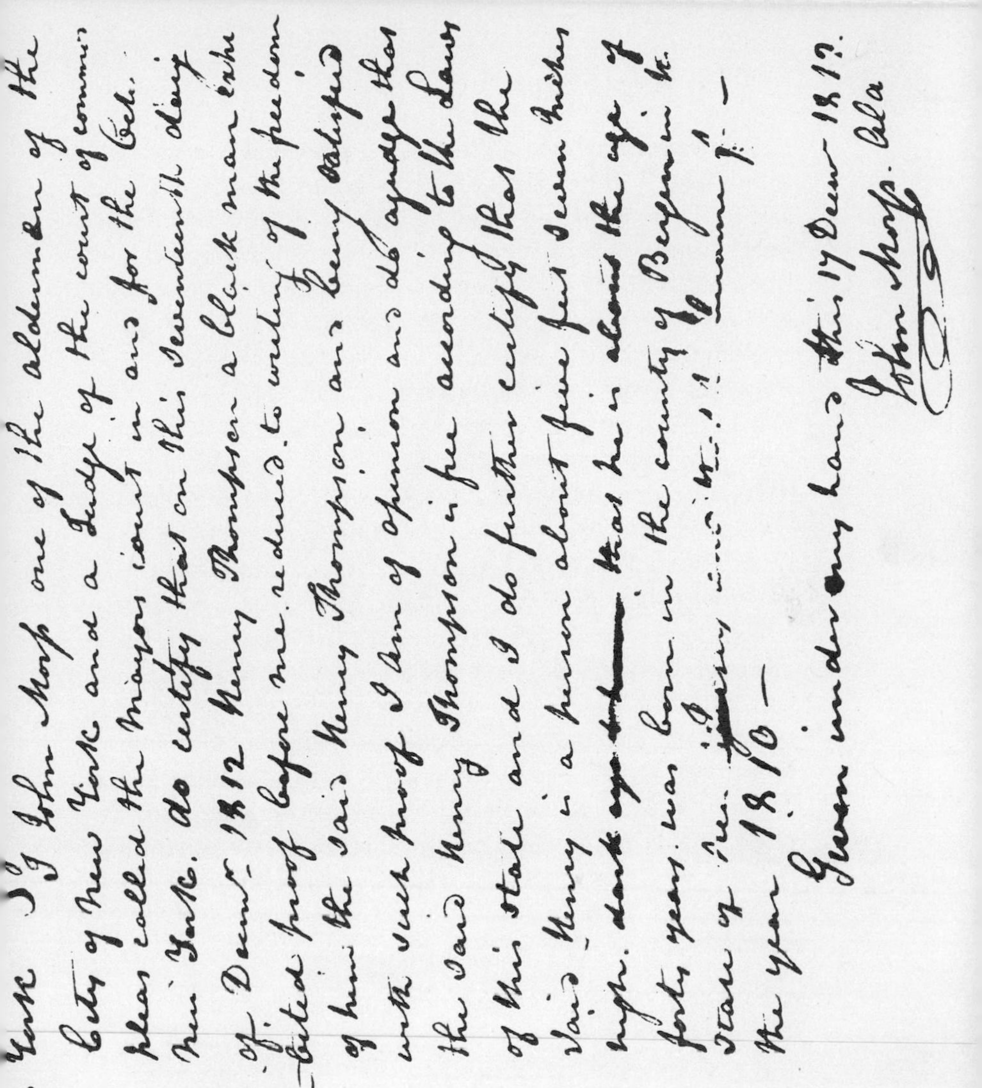

of New York

I John Sharp one of the aldermen of the City of New York and a Judge of the court of common pleas called the Mayors court in and for the City of New York do certify that on this Seventeenth day of Decem. 1812 Henry Thompson a black man exhibited proof before me reduced to writing of the freedom of him the said Henry Thompson an being satisfied with such proof I am of opinion and do adjudge that the said Henry Thompson is free according to the laws of this state and I do further certify that the said Henry is a person about five feet Seven inches high, dark complexion that he is about the age of forty years, was born in the county of Benjamin in the state of Free _____ in the year 1810 —

Given under my hand this 17 Decem 1812.

John Sharp. Ald

Figure 12.

Free blacks were often captured and sold back into slavery. Thus it helped to go before a judge—as Henry Thompson did on December 17, 1812—and get official confirmation of one's free status. Such a document would also help ensure the freedom of one's children. (*Collection of the author*)

Solomon Northup, a free black who was illegally kidnapped, did not have the handicaps that faced most slaves. He was literate and had a free family and friends in his home state of New York who would help him. But even with all these supposed advantages, it still took him twelve years to regain his freedom!

Communication proved to be Northup's major obstacle. While in a slave pen in Washington, D.C., he was beaten nearly to death for claiming to be a free man. The experience taught him that it was dangerous to let a prospective purchaser know that he was actually "hot property." So Northup kept his secret. His plan was to send a letter to friends in New York to solicit their help—a simple enough task. However, he lacked pen and paper and access to a post office. Were it ever discovered that he knew how to read and write, he would be punished, and the punishment would be more severe if he were caught actually writing to someone. Not until he had been with one master for ten years did Northup meet a white man he could trust. The man wrote the letters himself and mailed them to Northup's friends, who then acted quickly on his behalf.

RUNAWAY SLAVE ADS

Runaway slave advertisements provide vital information for black genealogists. The broadsides and posters were distributed to taverns, displayed on trees, walls, any place that guaranteed a lot of attention. Abolitionists and the free blacks in a community often destroyed these posters. But bounty hunting was a profitable and flourishing business. Occasionally, if the reward was sufficiently enticing, even a greedy free black would reveal the whereabouts of an unfortunate slave.

$100 REWARD.

Ran away from the subscriber, living eight miles from Baltimore, on Falls turnpike road, on Tuesday 22d July, 1814,

Negro Job,

He is a stout black man, about 35 years of age, 5 feet 10 or eleven inches high, stoops when walking fast, flat footed and turns his toes out when in the act of walking, stutters a little in common conversation, but when alarmed increases it—a lump or mark on his shin occasioned by a kick from a horse, has no whiskers and but a small beard—he is fond of dress and occasionally wears a watch, he also is fond of company, and if he drinks any spirits is very apt to use words which he doth not understand the signification of—and amongst his companions he is very noisy, calls himself Joseph Chew—he was seen in the neighborhood of York Haven, about the 1st of January 1817, has been employed by John Gross near York Haven and by John Shelly, on Shelly's island, but he may have left that.

I will give the above reward if he is secured in any jail so that I get him again, and all reasonable charges if brought home or lodged in Baltimore jail.

THOMAS JOHNSON.

Rockland, July 20, 1819.

Figure 13. ──────────────────────────────

A runaway slave poster, distributed locally because Job was thought to be in hiding not far from his master in Rockland, Maryland.
(Collection of the author)

Each ad generally included a description of the escaped slave, the name of the owner, amount of reward offered, and any other incidental fact that might help the owner retrieve his human property—whether the runaway was crippled, had a scar or brand, was defiant or obedient, spoke other languages, was accompanied by others, or had a particular skill. For example, some slaves were trained as "phlebotomists"—bleeders who drew blood as a medical technique for healing. Many runaway slaves were from cities where they had been hired out as artisans in a variety of trades. The runaway's skill in carpentry or metal working might be noted in the advertisements, of which the following are typical examples:

> Advertisements Appearing in the *Pennsylvania Gazette:*
> Run away on the 4th INST., At night from James Leonard in Middlesex County, East New Jersey, A Negro man named Simon, aged 40 years, is well-set fellow, about 5 feet 10 inches high, has large Eyes, and a Foot 12 inches long; he was bred and born in this Country, talks good English, can read and write, is very slow in speech, Can Bleed and Draw Teeth Pretending to Be a Great Doctor and Very Religious, and says He's A Churchman, Had on a dark grey Broadcloth Coat, with good apparel, and peeked toe'd Shoes. He took with him a Black Horse, about 13 Hands and Half-high, a Star in Forehead, branded with 2 on the near Thigh or Shouldre, and trots; also a black hunting Saddle about half worn. Whoever takes up and secures the said Negro, so that his Master may have him again shall have three pounds reward and reasonable charges, paid by James Leonard Sept. 11, 1740.

Run away 21st of August, from the Subscribers, of
Kingsess, Philadelphia County, A White Man and A
Negro, It is Supposed They are Gone Together, the
white Man's Name is Abraham Josep, a Yorkshire
Man, a Shoemaker by Trade aged about 24 Years.
The Negro's Name is Tom, a yellowish Colour,
pretty much pitted with Small Pox, thick set. Two
nights before there were several things stolen, and it
is suppossed they have them.

James Hunt
Peter Elliot
Sept. 10, 1741

Run away from the Sloop Sparrow, lately arrived
from Barbadoes, Joseph Perry Commander, a Negro
Man named John; he was born in Dominica and
Speaks French, But very Little English, he is a very
ill-featured Fellow, and has been much cut in his
back by often Whippings his Clothing was only a
Frock and Trowsers. Whoever bring him to John
Yeats, Merchant in Philadelphia, shall have Twenty
Shillings Reward, and reasonable Charges, paid by
John Yeats.

July 4, 1745

Run away the 2nd Instant, from John Pawling, at
Perkiomen, a likely lusty, Negroe Man, Named
Toney, 6 Foot high, about 24 Years of Age, Speaks
Good English and High Dutch [German]. Had on
when he went away, a striped Linsey Woolsey
Jacket, Tow Shirt and Trowsers, and Old Felt Hat,
Whoever takes up and secures him again shall have
Twenty-five Shillings Reward and reasonable
Charges paid by John Pawling.

June 5, 1746

> Run away on the 16th of July from Thomas Rutter,
> of this city a Negro Man, named Dick, commonly
> Called Preaching Dick, aged about 27 Years.
>
> Thomas Rutter
> Sept. 4, 1746

To find advertisements of runaways and slaves offered for sale, it is necessary to know the state where the slave was held. Check the historical society or university library of that state. In some instances, ads have been preserved in their original form, or they have been put on microfilm. It takes a great deal of time to browse through these records; the more information you have on the locale and period when a relative might have escaped from slavery, the more productive your search will be.

Newspapers are another prime research tool, since many southern plantation owners placed detailed ads in northern papers when slaves escaped, hoping to cut off their flight to freedom. The *Pennsylvania Gazette* is a particularly good source for such ads.

THE UNDERGROUND RAILROAD

The Railroad, a secret and complex network of free blacks, former slaves, and white abolitionists, helped many slaves escape from the South. Without it, few of the escapees who had worked their way north would have managed to survive. Siebert's *From Slavery to Freedom* includes thousands of names of station keepers and some of the passengers. In addition to these books, some libraries with collections on slavery have received documents and wills of other people who participated in the Underground Railroad.

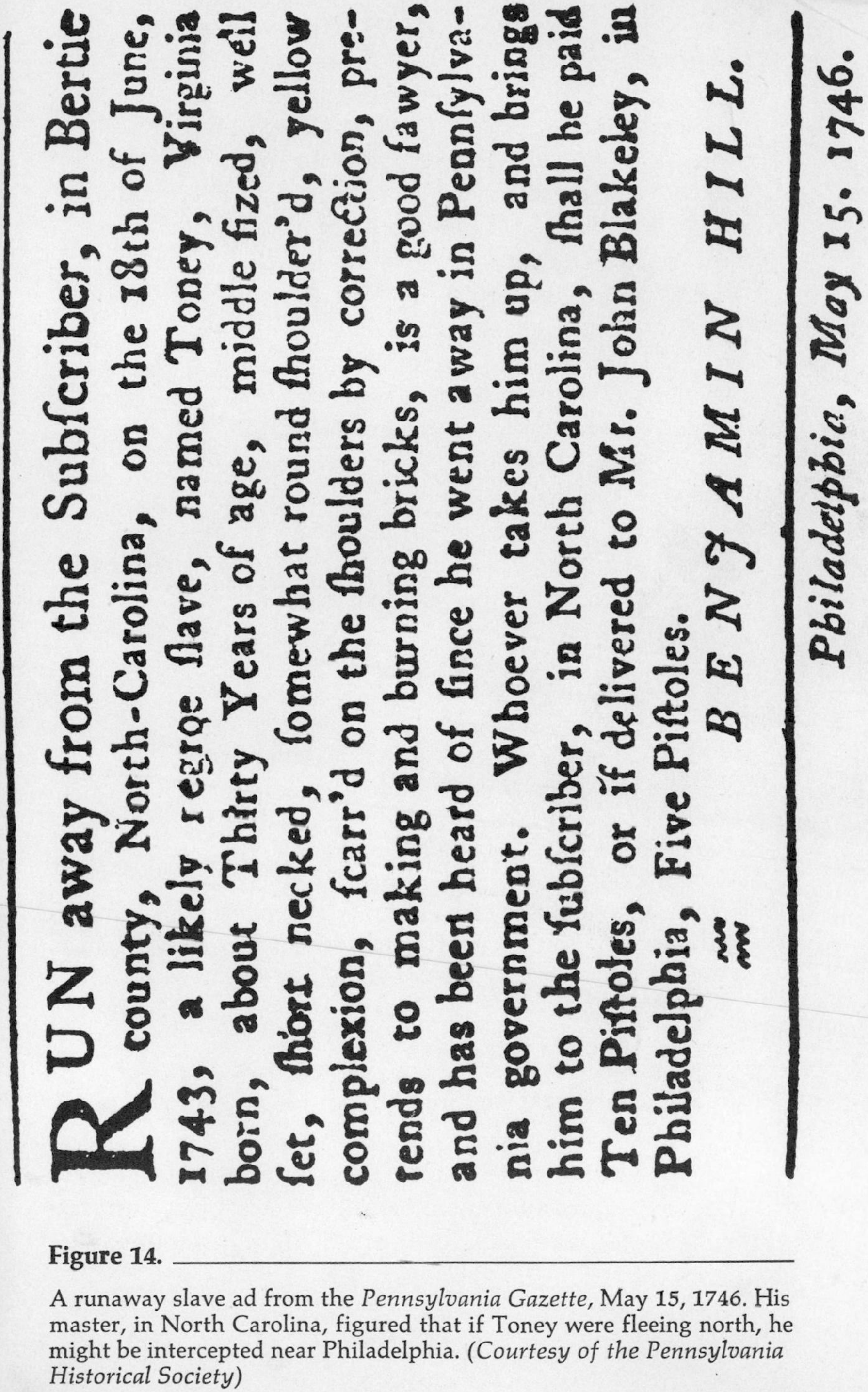

RUN away from the Subfcriber, in Bertie county, North-Carolina, on the 18th of June, 1743, a likely regro flave, named Toney, Virginia born, about Thirty Years of age, middle fized, well fet, fhort necked, fomewhat round fhoulder'd, yellow complexion, fcarr'd on the fhoulders by correction, pretends to making and burning bricks, is a good fawyer, and has been heard of fince he went away in Pennfylvania government. Whoever takes him up, and brings him to the fubfcriber, in North Carolina, fhall he paid Ten Piftoles, or if delivered to Mr. John Blakekey, in Philadelphia, Five Piftoles.

BENJAMIN HILL.

Philadelphia, May 15. 1746.

Figure 14.

A runaway slave ad from the *Pennsylvania Gazette*, May 15, 1746. His master, in North Carolina, figured that if Toney were fleeing north, he might be intercepted near Philadelphia. *(Courtesy of the Pennsylvania Historical Society)*

Since a great deal of secrecy was essential for the protection of escaped slaves, most people who worked with the Underground Railroad kept no written records. Luckily, William Still did and eventually published them in his book, *The Underground Railroad*.

I was delighted to find my own name in Still's book. In 1858 Jacob Blockson, my great-grandfather's cousin, escaped from Jesse W. Layton near Seaford, Delaware, and went north with three other fugitive slaves. They were directed to Still's office in Philadelphia. Still, who kept records of all the fugitives who came to the Anti-Slavery Office, describes Jacob Blockson as "a stout and healthy-looking man, about twenty-seven years of age, with a countenance indicative of having no sympathy with Slavery." On page 489 of his book, he quotes Blockson as saying:

> "I left, because I didn't want to stay with him any longer. My master was about to be sold out this Fall, and I made up my mind that I did not want to be sold like a horse, the way they generally sold darkies then; so when I started I resolved to die sooner than I would be taken back; this was my intention all the while. I left my wife, and one child; the wife's name was Lear [Leah] and the child was Alexander. I want to get them on soon too. I made some arrangements for their coming if I got off safe to Canada."

His cousin, my great-grandfather James, was already safely esconced in Canada. He had also escaped on The Railroad.

When blacks in the United States referred to "Heaven," it was not the North they meant but Canada. In the North, antiblack feelings ran high, educational and employment opportunities were limited, and black social life was severely restricted. Antiblack riots in Philadelphia, New York, Palmyra, Pittsburgh, Cincinnati, and other cities were violent indicators of how even northern whites felt. In some areas, blacks weren't allowed to settle at all. While many escaped slaves did settle in the northern states, the Underground Railroad lines didn't stop until they reached Canada— a final refuge from the law and from the various individuals who kidnapped blacks, even free ones, and sold them into slavery.

Migration to Canada reached its peak in the 1840's and 1850's with blacks, both slave and free, settling in southern Ontario communities then called Dawn, Colchester, Elgin, Dresden, Windsor, Sandwich, Bush, Wilberforce, Hamilton, St. Catherines, Chatham, Riley, Auberton, London, Malden, and Confield. Blacks had settled in Nova Scotia after the War of 1812, in an area later named Africville—conveniently located for farming and fishing, as well as for wage labor in Halifax.

The records of such black Canadian communities can be traced through a number of sources. If you know that a relative lived in a given town, the local historical society might be contacted for information about the particular time period he or she was there. Names and addresses of historical societies can be obtained from your local library. Information about land ownership · deeds can be obtained from the capitals of Canadian provinces. Abolitionist newspapers such as *The Liberator, The North Star,* and *The Voice of the Fugitive* carried news of black communities in Canada. More consistent information, though, was contained in *The Provincial Freeman,* edited by Mary Ann Shad, who lived in Canada and began the newspaper for blacks living there. Microfilm copies of this paper can be viewed at Pennsylvania State University.

William Still later received the following letter from Jacob Blockson. (I reproduce the original punctuation and spelling.)

Saint Catharines. Canada West,
Dec. 26, 1858

Mr. Still: Sir:—you will please Envelope this and send it to John Sheppard Bridgeville P. office in Sussex county Delaware, seal it in black and oblige me, write to her to come to you.

Dear Wife:—I now inform you I am in Canada and am well and hope you are the same, and would wish you to be here about next august, you come to suspension bridge and from there to St. Catharines, write and let me know. I am doing well working for a Butcher this winter, and will get good wages in the spring I now get $2.50 a week.

I Jacob Blockson, George Lewis, George Alligood and James Alligood are all in St. Catharines, and met George Ross from Lewis Wright's, Jim Blockson [my great-grandfather], Lea Ann Blockson, my son Alexander & Lewis and Ames will be here and Isabella also, if you cant bring all bring Alexander surely, write when you will come and I will meet you in Albany. Love to you all, from your loving Husband,   Jacob Blockson
fare through $12.30 to here.

Leah did not go to Canada to join her husband; during the Civil War he returned to Seaford Hundred, Delaware, where they spent the rest of their lives. Leah died in 1894. *Hundred* was an old English term for a division of land containing one hundred able-bodied

men, which indicates that our slave family was one of
the original hundred in that area.

Ironically, as in Leah and Jacob Blockson's case, the
overwhelming desire to be free added to the breakdown
of black family life. At times, families had to make the
agonizing decision of flight for a few or continued
slavery for all. There was always the vague hope that
the refugees would be able to rescue those who stayed
behind. But all agreed that it was better for some to be
free and some slave than for all to remain forever
chained.

So it must have been for Cidney Still whose husband
purchased his freedom and went to New Jersey. Cidney
escaped with her four young children to join him and
lived in New Jersey for several months until she was
captured and returned to slavery. Knowing she couldn't
escape with four children a second time, she left behind
the two older ones and took her infant daughters back
to the Piney Woods. There the Stills settled, engaging in
small farming, wood chopping, cranberry picking, and
other jobs in order to support their family, which
eventually grew to eighteen children. The youngest,
William, became the well-known Philadelphia antislavery
worker mentioned earlier. His mother could take
comfort in the knowledge that, although she had been
forced to leave two sons in slavery, another son helped
scores of other blacks reach freedom.

The literature is filled with heartbreaking accounts
of people searching for family members. Isaac Williams,
born into slavery, had been separated from his mother
at an early age and for years knew nothing of her
whereabouts. Only by accident did he meet a cousin of
his mother's who eventually identified the plantation
where Williams' mother had been sold. Williams, who

had purchased his own freedom and become a minister in Detroit, offered four hundred dollars for his mother. His offer was initially turned down but eventually accepted: in 1857 sixty-year-old "Aunt Sally" went to Detroit—as a free woman—to live with her son. At that time she did not know the whereabouts of her husband or another son; she had heard that a third son had been imprisoned after an attempted escape from slavery.

Moses Grandy, after purchasing his own freedom, worked odd jobs to save enough money to buy his wife and son. When his *Narrative of the Life of Moses Grandy* was published, two of his daughters had already purchased their own freedom and Grandy was attempting to locate and purchase his other children.

Some families could never be reunited, but at least they retained some knowledge of their origins. Gustavus Vassa's memory of his homeland was rich. Of all existing narratives, his provides the fullest descriptions of life in his native land. He grew up in Benin, now part of Nigeria, and gives interesting details of the customs of those times.

Venture Smith was another of the fortunate few who could describe his background. In his 1797 narrative he states:

> I was born at Dukandarra, in Guinea, about the year 1729. My father's name was Saugm Furro, Prince of the tribe of Dukandara. My father had three wives. Polygamy was not uncommon in that country, especially among the rich, as every man was allowed to keep as many wives as he could maintain. By his first wife he had three children. The eldest of them was myself, named by my father, Broteer. The other two were named Cundazo and Soozaduka. My father had two children by his

second wife, and one by his third. I descended from
a very large, tall and stout race of beings, much
larger than the generality of people in other parts of
the globe, being commonly considerable above six
feet in height, and every way well proportioned.

Nancy Prince, a free black woman born in Massachusetts, wrote of her background in 1856 with the
publication of *A Narrative of the Life and Travels of
Mrs. Nancy Prince:*

I was born in Newburyport, September the 15th,
1759. My mother was born in Gloucester,
Massachusetts—the daughter of Tobias Wornton,
or Backus, so called. He was stolen from Africa
when a lad and was a slave of Captain Winthrop
Sargent; but although a slave, he fought for liberty.
He was in the Revolutionary army and at the battle
of Bunker Hill. He often used to tell us, when little
children, the evils of Slavery, and how he was
stolen from his native land. My grandmother was
an Indian of this country; she became a captive to
the English, or their descendants. She served as a
domestic in the Parsons family. My father, Thomas
Gardner, was born in Nantucket; his parents were
of African descent. He died in Newburyport, when
I was three years old. My mother was thus a second
time widow, with her two children, and she
returned to Gloucester to her father. My mother
married her third husband, by whom she had six
children. My stepfather was stolen from Africa, and
while the vessel was at anchor in one of our Eastern
ports, he succeeded in making his escape from his
captors, by swimming ashore. I have often heard
him tell the tale.

Other black writers can provide only hints. John

Brown, who had been a slave in South Carolina, simply
states that his father was stolen from Africa. But for the
vast majority, whether slave or free, the roots were
simply unknown. It was the exception rather than the
rule for one to be able to draft a family tree. Family
members had little way of knowing most of their
relatives and therefore no way of tracing as far back as
perhaps even one generation. Besides, searching for
immediate family members was of far greater urgency
than tracing ancestry, however deep the longing to do
so. The enormity of the problem can only be appreciated
if you remember that stories of people like Isaac
Williams and Moses Grandy represent only a few that
were published. The vast majority of uprooted people
were never identified by recorded history.

Lincoln declared the Emancipation Proclamation on
January 1, 1863, but it was not until December 18, 1865,
eight months after the close of the Civil War, that the
Thirteenth Amendment to the Constitution *officially*
ended slavery in the United States. But no legislation
could ever erase the devastation slavery had wrought on
the black people. It had effectively stripped its victims
of their power to participate in a normal, civilized
society and almost wrecked the black family, the very
foundation of that society.

Emancipation, many slaves thought, would change all
that, allowing them to live as human beings again, build
strong families, educate their children. But one hundred
years ago, few of them could have foreseen the century
of struggle, sacrifice, and incredible suffering blacks had
to endure to win even their basic rights as American
citizens. After emancipation, the reunion of separated
families was still difficult at best, and numerous factors
continued to work against family stability. For black

Americans, the search for identity and dignity would
continue for generations to come.

The destruction of slavery produced two immediate,
almost instinctive, responses. The first reaction of many
former slaves was to move—as vital a step in testing the
reality of freedom as it was in finding better living
conditions. In later years, many blacks migrated north
in search of economic opportunity that the near-slave
conditions of the South did not bring.

For many, the second immediate response to freedom
was to change their names. Some wanted to shed their
master's own surname. Others, called Big Buck, Mammy,
Cuff (a name derived from "handcuff," often given
to defiant or runaway slaves) or a classical name like
Pompey or Caesar, later wanted to adopt more
conventional names. But geographical relocation and
name changes have added to our research problems.
There are few records to tell us that Cato of Mississippi
and John Thompson of Ohio were the same person.

Genealogical obstacles mounted as white society
closed its doors to blacks. Segregation and racism closed
off access to public and many private resources. Court
records of births, deaths, and marriages were inaccessible
to most black people. Public libraries often didn't exist
for blacks—in some cities, there was a small and inferior
Colored Branch or Colored Department of the public
library. Southerners, although not particularly
concerned about equality, were always interested in
separation.

Not until 1952 did a public library in the South open
its main facility to blacks. Of course, not all blacks were
equipped with the literacy that enabled a man like
Richard Wright to use references sources. The long
years of being denied an education had left their scars.

Nevertheless, the problems of immediate post-

Emancipation name changes, segregation, and enforced illiteracy are in some ways lessened because of the extent and detail of records during this period—far more and far better records than you will ever find for the slave years.

FREEDMEN'S BUREAU

The Freedmen's Bureau was established by the federal government just before the close of the Civil War to assist the newly emancipated slaves adjust to freedom. The bureau's activities were confined primarily to the former Confederate states, border states, and the District of Columbia. Unfortunately, it was remarkably short-lived—it had virtually stopped functioning at all by 1869 and was discontinued in 1872. All unfinished work was later transferred to the Freedmen's Branch in the Adjutant General's office, where bureau records continue to be housed.

Most of the records have been placed on microfilm and are available to researchers through the National Archives. They include letters to the bureau commissioner, school reports, assistant commissioners' reports, and a variety of orders and circulars. Despite the fairly extensive collection, locating information on specific individuals can be difficult. If possible, ask for help from personnel familiar with the materials.

If you know or suspect that a family member was a depositor in the Freedmen's Savings and Trust Company, which operated from 1865 to 1874, it would be worth your while to examine *Registers of Signatures of Depositions in Branches of the Freedmen's Savings and Trust Company, 1865–1874*, a microfilm publication available from the National Archives. The registers are

arranged alphabetically by name of state, then city
where the branch was located, then by date when the
account was established, then account number. Many
numbers are missing, a few are out of order, and in
some cases blocks of numbers were not used. Many
registers are missing. But despite these difficulties,
valuable information can be obtained. Many registers
include name of depositor, date of entry, place of birth,
place brought up, residence, age, complexion, name of
employer and/or occupation, wife or husband, children,
father, mother, brothers, sisters, remarks, and signature.
Early registers also include the name of the former
owner and name of the plantation. Some entries include
a copy of the death certificate.

By this point in your research, you will most likely
have run into one problem we haven't treated yet—
miscegenation, the mixing of blacks with whites and
other races. I've delayed a treatment of this important
problem until this point because it's such a complex one
that it can make even the best research seem futile. But
a full discussion of what miscegenation is and how
greatly it affects genealogies will help you fill in some of
the gaps in your burgeoning family tree.

Chapter Six

MISCEGENATION

Merriam-Webster dispassionately defines "miscegenation" as "a mixture of races; *esp*: marriage or cohabitation between a white person and a member of another race."

Derived from the Latin words *miscere* (to mix) and *genus* (race), the term itself was coined in 1864 by David G. Croly and George Wakeman in their pamphlet, *Miscegenation: The Theory of the Blending of the Races Applied to the American White Man and Negro*. The publication caused quite a stir among abolitionists, southern planters, and politicians.

Why such shocked reaction? Certainly not because such racial mixing was unheard of. It was actually as much a part of plantation life as slavery itself. People were simply loathe to bring such dirty linen into the open.

It was a subject so fraught with explosive feelings— *on both sides*—that society tried to ignore what many members casually accepted in private. Such shame is not such an old-fashioned virtue either—even today, miscegenation is an issue so sensitive that many blacks and whites refuse to discuss it. But away from the glare of publicity, knowledgeable people admitted that such mixing was simply another part of everyday life. Southern white women, in fact, provide some of the most poignant examples of its effect.

President James Madison's sister, for instance, once remarked to the Reverend George Brown, a Presbyterian minister in Virginia, that "we Southern ladies are complimented with names of wives, but we are only mistresses of seraglios."

Frances Kemble wrote, "Any lady is ready to tell you who is the father of all the mulatto children in everybody's household but her own. These, she seems to think, drop from the clouds."

Ellen Craft, born a slave in Georgia, was given as a wedding gift to her own white half-sister. Her master's wife did not want Ellen in her own house where she would be constantly reminded that Ellen was her husband's child.

Southern divorce records attest to the prevalence of women filing for divorce for this very reason— sometimes naming slave women as correspondents. And it's important to realize that the white man's custom of "climbing the back fences" didn't end after the Civil War. In *Killers of the Dream*, in which Lillian Smith describes her white southern upbringing during the 1920's, she says most white women quickly learned that "discrimination was a word with secret meanings and they did not like its secrets. In the white southern woman's dictionary, it could be defined as a painful way of life which too often left an empty place in her bed and an ache in her heart."

History certainly doesn't lack for other famous examples of such affairs. William Wells Brown states that his maternal grandmother was a descendant of Daniel Boone. In his 1890 book, *How the Way Was Prepared*, Calvin Fairbanks states that Patrick Henry, the orator who delivered the famous "Give me liberty or give me death" speech, had a black son named Melancthon. According to Edward Turner's *The Negro in Pennsylvania*, Benjamin Franklin kept slave concubines during his younger years. As the famous man grew older, though, he joined the Pennsylvania Abolitionist Society and forswore slavery. But no one can say for certain that he threw off sleeping with black women as well. Thomas Jefferson, third President of the United States and author of the Declaration of Independence, sired a number of mulatto children— by his dead wife's half sister.

Jefferson was a fairly substantial slaveholder. One of the documents he left is a list of fifty-two of his slaves, probably those to be vaccinated, written in March 1826. Since he was having some financial problems at the time, the list could also have been prepared for a sale. Jefferson listed the name of each slave's mother after each slave name, in chronological order (from 1816 to 1823). Two small groups are headed "Tufton" and "Lego"—possibly a reference to their origins. A number of Jefferson's mulatto children are listed—Burwell, Joe Fessel, John Hemings, Madison and Eston Hemings. The last three were probably a result of his long-standing affair with Sally Hemings, his half-sister-in-law. Madison lived and died in Washington, D.C. Another son died in the Civil War.

Jefferson's relationship with "Black Sal," as Sally Hemings was often known, has long been a sticky problem for historians, many of whom refuse to believe that it ever occurred at all. Yet the truth of the allegation was rarely disputed during his lifetime—several of Sally's children bore such a striking resemblance to the President that few doubted their paternity. Evidence from other sources, including Jefferson's own *Farm Book*, seems to support the opinion of Jefferson's contemporaries.

Public interest in such famous indiscretions never seemed to wane. An 1845 issue of the *Cleveland American* newspaper reported: "We are incredibly informed that a natural son of Jefferson by the celebrated 'Black Sal,' a person of no little renown in the politics of 1800 and thereafter, is now living in a central county of Ohio. We shall endeavor to get at the truth of the matter and make public the result of our inquiries." (They never did.)

Stephen Girard, a wealthy shipping merchant, spent most of his time in Philadelphia but also owned thirty slaves in New Orleans. His controversial will set aside a large portion of his fortune for an orphanage for poor white boys, thus giving a rather obvious clue to his feelings about blacks. But the first person actually mentioned in the will was Hannah, Girard's housekeeper and his brother's black mistress. Girard provided money for her until the day she died. The will, incidentally, was finally broken after one of the longest court fights in Pennsylvania history, and Girard's orphanage was forced to admit blacks.

Even members of the South Carolina legislature were forced to recognize miscegenation as a fact of life. When they tried to define race by suggesting a Negro was any person with even a single drop of nonwhite blood, George Tillman objected. "Gentlemen," he solemnly declared, "then we must acknowledge that there is not a full-blooded Caucasian on the floor of this convention!"

Which means that most blacks involved in genealogical research will simply have to come to terms with the high degree of miscegenation that has occurred in America. Sooner or later, your family tree will finally reveal a couple of white members. If it does, you'll often find that *their* family records will turn up valuable clues for you.

Some of the success I have had in tracing my own family, for example, can be directly attributed to the records I found concerning the white branch of the family. From a book on the genealogy of the white Blocksons, I learned that they came to this country from Scotland early in the seventeenth century and founded the town of Bloxom in Accomack County, Virginia. The town still exists today. One branch of the family went to Seaford, Sussex County, Delaware, where they became seamen, doctors, and farmers.

John Blockson moved from Virginia to Delaware and in 1790 owned seven slaves and 361 acres of land. My family descended from slaves owned by this white family, although it is not known if we originated during his residence in Virginia or in Delaware. We are listed among the oldest black slave families in Sussex County. So far, after extensive research in the Delaware Hall of Records, I've been able to trace them back five generations. I've even found records of land owned by my great-great-grandfather in the late eighteenth century and am still hoping this source will help me trace my family back to Africa.

As another example, there are many black Lee families in Virginia, since so many blacks took that surname after General Richard Henry Lee, the Revolutionary War hero and an ancestor of another famous general—Robert E. Therefore, blacks researching this name, would also have to do quite a bit of genealogy covering the white Lees in order to trace their own family.

Many black families with the name of Randolph, especially those in the Ohio area, can trace their lineage back to the Randolphs of Virginia. The Randolphs were one of the first families of that state, a genteel clan that owned sprawling estates and hundreds of slaves and took an active part in colonial politics. Thomas Jefferson and John Marshall were just two of their famous cousins.

John Randolph, the family patriarch, liberated his 385 slaves when he died. Most of these slaves settled in Ohio's Mercer County. After a long period of often violent white opposition, they wound up near the towns of Piqua and Troy. Many of them retained the name of

Randolph as a mark of gratitude for the man who freed them.

But the Randolphs acquired a less savory reputation in the years to come. And in 1792, a scandal tainted their name for good. On October 1 of that year, Richard Randolph's sister-in-law, Ann Cary Randolph (known as Nancy), allegedly gave birth to a child.

Slaves present at the birth claimed that Richard killed the child, depositing it on some old shingles—probably because, many of them assumed, he had also fathered it. Richard demanded a trial to clear his name, hired John Marshall and Patrick Henry to defend him, and won the case.

As rumors spread from plantation to plantation, one of the stories that began to gain more frequency was that the child was really killed because its father was black. From this incident emerged the term "nigger in the woodpile." The term also referred to the slaves' gleeful interest in such gossip and indicated that they couldn't keep a secret.

Although whites might well have avoided admitting the possibility of Negro blood in their veins, black families often reminisced about their famous white relatives. Such reminiscing was sometimes written down, giving us an excellent source for tracing our families down to and through the white branches. Because of such records, for example, many black families still living in Pennsylvania can trace their ancestry directly back to the slaves of William Penn, the state's founder.

Biographies of such whites can often fill in a number of gaping holes in your research. The history of James Varick, one of the founders and the first bishop of the African Methodist Episcopal Zion Church, has been preserved through just such a family chronicle,

B. F. Wheeler's *The Varick Family* (Mobile, 1906):

Richard Varick, who was of Dutch descent, the
father of James Varick, was born in Hackensack,
New Jersey, but when a child moved with his
parents to New York City. It is difficult to tell to
what nationality James Varick belongs. At least
three different nationalities enter into his compositon.
Through his veins flowed the blood of Negro, the
American Indian, and the Dutchman. According to
the American way of settling race identity, I suppose
he would be called a Negro, for he had Negro blood
flowing through his veins. . . The exact date of
Varick's birth is not clearly known, but, putting all
the facts of his eventful life together, it appears that
1750 is as near a date as can be given as the year of
his birth. . . . He was born in stirring times when
the best brains and the best blood were all aflame
with a desire for liberty, which was expressed
twenty-six years after his birth in the Declaration of
Independence of English rule. Varick caught the
spirit of his age and in due time was ready to lead
his little band of followers to religious liberty. Just
where Varick was born is not clearly known. It is
stated by the early fathers of the church that he was
born in Newburg [sic], New York, up the Hudson
River from New York City. While Varick was born
in Newburg, it appears that his mother was a
resident of New York and was in Newburg on a visit
when Varick was born. At any rate, James Varick
was reared in New York City. His mother was a
colored woman of very bright complexion. Whether
she had been a slave or was a free woman is not
known. In the history of New York City the rich
and distinguished Varick family has figured most
conspicuously in its social, political and commercial
life for the last two centuries. One of the members

of this cultured Varick family was mayor of New
York City. The Varick Bank of New York City is
named in honor of, and controlled by this same
strong and influential family. Varick Street on
which I have walked many times, which runs from
Clarkson Street to Canal, is also named after this
distinguished family. It is possible that Varick's
mother at one time was a slave in the family.

In any case, finding such white ancestors is certainly
nothing to be ashamed of—it happens in some of the
best families. Other famous men were themselves the
products of such dalliances or of mixed marriages. For
example, mystery still shrouds the births of Alexander
Hamilton, first Secretary of the Treasury, and John
James Audubon, who became famous for his bird
studies. Both were born in the West Indies and frequently
cited as the products of mixed parentage.

Samuel Fraunces, who founded the famous tavern in
New York City's Wall Street area, also came from a
West Indian mixed parentage. Fraunces was nicknamed
"Black Sam" and was proud of his heritage—he even
established a museum consisting of seventy miniature
figures representing a black Queen of Sheba bringing
presents to King Solomon. It was Fraunces' daughter
Phoebe who exposed the famous assassination plot
against George Washington, a frequent visitor to
Fraunces' Tavern.

Fraunces later moved to Philadelphia to establish
another tavern. It's assumed he died there, although he's
listed in the city directory until 1790. His New York
tavern is now owned and operated by the Sons of the
American Revolution. And despite all evidence to the
contrary, some historians won't allow us to claim him
as one of our own—they insist he was white.

Another famous Philadelphian, Robert Purvis, was born in South Carolina of Jewish, Moorish, and English parentage. After he was sent North to attend Amherst College, he decided to remain. Although Purvis could have passed for white, he refused to reject his mixed ancestry, as did his son Charles many years later. Purvis became extremely wealthy and was known as a powerful abolitionist speaker.

When the Pennsylvania legislature voted to disenfranchise its black citizens in 1838, Purvis issued an appeal and collected signatures as a protest. The original "Appeal of 40,000 Disenfranchised Citizens of Pennsylvania" is now housed in the Philadelphia Historical Society.

The Healy family is one of the more outstanding examples of just how much descendants of mixed parentage have given our country. Of the ten children born to the Irish immigrant father and black mother, most remained devout Roman Catholics throughout their lives. One of the brothers, James became the bishop of Portland, Maine, and an assistant to the Pope several months before his death. Another brother, Patrick, was the first black American to receive a Ph.D. degree. He became president of Georgetown University, the nation's oldest Catholic college, and was often referred to as its "second Founder."

While the sexual exploitation of black women was commonplace, as is readily acknowledged even by southern whites, mixed marriages were also not uncommon. They have been occurring, in fact, from the earliest colonial times.

Thomas Branagan, writing about late-eighteenth century Philadelphia, said:

There are many blacks . . . who will not be satisfied
unless they get white women for wives and are
likewise exceedingly impertinent to white people in
low circumstances. . . . I solemnly swear, I have
seen more white women married to, and deluded
through the acts of seduction by negroes in one year
in Philadelphia, than for the eight years I was
visiting the West Indies and Southern States.

I know a black man who seduced a young white
girl, who soon married him, and died with a broken
heart. On her death, he said that he would not
disgrace himself to have a negro wife and acted
accordingly, for soon after he married a white
woman. . . . There are perhaps hundreds of white
women thus fascinated by black men in this city,
and there are thousands of black children by them
at present.

Frederick Douglass, who was himself of mixed
parentage, caused quite a stir when he took a white
woman named Helen Pitts as his second wife. He later
stated that "I took as my first wife the race of my
mother and as my second wife the race of my father."

Such openness was extremely rare. But evidently it
worked. In an August 1884 letter to Amy Post,
Douglass wrote:

You will be happy to know that my marriage has
not diminished the number of invitations I used to
receive for lectures and speeches and that the
momentary breeze of popular disfavor caused by
my marriage has passed away. I have had very little
sympathy with the curiosity of the world about my
domestic relations. What business has the world
with the color of my wife?

Not all of Douglass' contemporaries were prepared to chance public censure by being too open or obvious. Thaddeus Stevens, the main architect of the Reconstruction period, fell in love with a mulatto woman named Lydie Smith, evidently a woman of superior beauty and ability. After the death of her black husband, by whom she had had two children, Stevens hired her as his housekeeper. In reality, Lydie presided over all of Stevens' households as any wife would. Friends even referred to her as "Mrs. Stevens." But although they were devoted to each other, they never did get married. Stevens was already in enough trouble for proposing that the land of former slaveholders be divided and given to the blacks who had worked it as slaves.

Probably the sole reason for the decline of such marriages, especially in the South, was the series of primitive "black laws" many colonies devised to legislate them out of existence. And though intermarriage is quite prevalent today and few people worry much about how "pure" their blood is, some of these black laws are still on the books.

Sometimes the offspring of mixed marriages founded entire communities, such as Gouldtown in New Jersey. The people of Gouldtown are descendants of the wealthy, powerful, and white Fenwick family. In the 1670's one of the Fenwick heiresses, Elizabeth Adams, married a black servant. Her grandfather, John Fenwick, threatened to cut her off from the family wealth "unless the Lord open her eyes to see the abominable transgression against His name and her good father, by giving her true repentance and forsaking that Black which hath been the ruin of her." There is no evidence that she ever repented, but the family grew and prospered.

Others joined this growing family. From the West Indies came two mulatto brothers by the name of Pierce. They married two Dutch sisters, Marie and Hannah Van Aca. The Murrays, who claimed to be descendants of a Swedish woman and a Lenape Indian, settled down in the new community. A white woman whose husband was killed during the French and Indian War married his black slave Cuff. They also joined this mulatto community, which over the years intermarried so extensively that just about everybody was related to everybody else.

Many Gouldtowners have achieved prominence in black society and are still powerful in New Jersey today. Reuben Cuff, whose wife was a Gould, moved to Philadelphia and became one of the organizers of the African Methodist Church. To be sure, a considerable number of other Gouldtowners have since burned their bridges behind them and quietly melted into the white population.

Another example of such group mixing was nineteenth century New Orleans, which was nevertheless quite conscious and protective of the resulting class divisions. Blacks of mixed parentage were placed in rigid categories, strictly according to the racial makeup of their parents. The following list goes from lowest class to highest, as the amount of black blood declines proportionately from term to term:

Parents	Child
black and white	Mulatto
mulatto and white	Quadroon
quadroon and white	Octoroon
mulatto and mulatto	Cascos
mulatto and black	Sambo
sambo and black	Mango

octoroon and white	Mustifee
mustifee and white	Mustifino

One of the most interesting groups that evolved from such a mixed society was labeled the *Cordon Bleu*, a class of wealthy free blacks who were products of French/black liaisons. Many of the black women, left fortunes by their French lovers, used their newfound wealth to send their children to France for an education and to acquire large plantations and slaves. Creoles were noted for not working their slaves as hard as Americans, but also had a reputation for not feeding or clothing them as generously.

The offspring—those who became known as *Cordon Bleus*—were ostracized by New Orleans society, scorned by whites, and alienated from other blacks largely because of their education. When they returned from Paris, they therefore tended to gravitate toward one another. Armand Lanusse gathered a group of them together and became known as their unofficial leader and spokesman. They called themselves Les Cenelles, or the hollyberries. In 1845, Lanusse' group published the first black poetry anthology in the United states titled, appropriately enough, *Les Cenelles*.

Mixed marriages often helped to weaken black family ties even further. Not all black partners rejected their past, but many tried. The resulting rejection or actual destruction of records erected one more barrier for descendants in search of family. It is a painful subject for blacks, but one we need to face if we are to pull our family histories together.

PASSING

From very early times in the United States, blacks have been conscious of class divisions among themselves.

During slavery, fair–skinned blacks were often employed as house servants and developed a feeling of superiority over field blacks. The early association of light skin with greater privilege resulted in large numbers of blacks passing for white and cutting ties with their former associates.

Blacks passed for a variety of reasons; some just to escape the oppression of being black in the United States.

From the *New Orleans Picayune:*

> *TWO HUNDRED DOLLARS REWARD.*—Ran away from the subscriber, (18) November, *a white negro man*, about thirty-five years old, hight about five feet eight or ten inches, blue eyes, has a yellow woolly head, very fair skin (particularly under his clothes). . . . Said negro man was raised in Columbia, S.C., and is well known by the name of Cuff Frazier. . . . He was lately known to be working on the road in Alabama, near Moore's Turnout, and *passed as a white man*, by the name of Jesse Teams. I will give the above reward, &c.
>
> J. D. Allen
Barnwell Court House, S.C.
>
> P.S.—Said man has a good-shaped foot and leg; and his foot is very small and hollow.

From the *Savannah Republican*, Oct. 8, 1855:

> *FIFTY DOLLARS REWARD.*—Ran away from the subscriber, on the 22d ulto., my negro man, Albert, who is 27 years old, *very white, so much so that he would not be suspected of being a negro.* Has blue eyes, and very light hair. Wore, when he left, a long thin beard, and rode a chestnut sorrel horse, with about $70 belonging to himself.

He is about five feet eight inches high, and weighs
about 150 pounds. Has a very humble and meek
appearance; can neither read nor write, and is a
very kind and amiable fellow; speaks much like a
low country negro. He has, no doubt, been led off
by some miserable wretch, during my absence in
New York.

The above reward will be paid for his delivery to
me, or to Savannah, or for his apprehension and
confinement in Bethel jail where I can get him.

I.M.
Bethel, Glynn Co., Ga.

From the *Richmond* (Virginia) *Whig:*

ONE HUNDRED DOLLARS REWARD will be
given for the apprehension of my negro, Edmund
Kenney. He has straight hair, and complexion so
nearly white that it is believed a stranger would
suppose there was no African blood in him. He was
with my boy Dick, a short time in Norfolk, and
offered him for sale, and was apprehended, but
escaped under pretense of being a white man.

Anderson Bowles

In a daring escape, Ellen Craft posed as a southern
planter, while her darker-skinned husband acted as her
servant. Both arrived safely in Philadelphia, having
stayed in fine southern hotels along their way. But as
soon as possible, Ellen Craft resumed her true identity.

Other blacks passed for other reasons. Walter White,
one-time director of the NAACP, passed during certain
times of his life in order to obtain the information he
needed. Fair-skinned and blue-eyed, White never shed
his identification as a black person, but he took
advantage of his ease in passing by traveling throughout
the South to observe the treatment of blacks in many

situations, notably in the Armed Forces and as victims
of lynch mobs. The facts he gathered were added to the
voluminous NAACP files, most of which are now
available in the Library of Congress.

With the advantages open to pure-blooded whites, it
was only natural that some blacks should attempt to
look as white as possible. The result was such cosmetics
as skin bleaches, hair straighteners, special makeup—
and an admiration for those with skin naturally light
enough to earn the label "high yellow."

As if there weren't already enough discrimination
from whites, black people often formed their own class
lines based on color. Many cities had their black Four
Hundred, or "leading families," or black bourgeoisie—
a term of E. Franklin Frazier. No matter what the label,
the highest social life was for the fair-skinned.
Sometimes light-skinned children were even given
preferential treatment within their own families. In
Washington, D.C., a well-known "blue vein" church
catered to light-skinned black members. It was felt that
if one's veins showed blue, then the skin was light
enough to rank one among the elite. The quarter moon
on one's fingernails was another indication of favorably
light skin color. Dark-skinned blacks sometimes married
lighter-skinned women, saying they were "preparing
for their children."

Such discrimination has been prevalent in black life
for a long time and has added to the difficulties of the
black genealogist, for it is one more factor in the
separation of families. It has also been a source of
bitterness toward light-skinned blacks who turned their
backs on the darker-skinned or looked down on them.
Usually, however, black people didn't expose those they
knew to be passing, no matter how much they might
have envied or hated them.

Why? Because exposure brought almost certain and swift censure, including loss of job and spouse. Such cases commonly made the newspapers. One that received considerable attention was the Kip Rhinelander case in the 1920's. Alice Jones, whose father was black, had married a white man and was eventually led to court and forced to strip to the waist in an attempt to prove that she was black.

What is black in one country, of course, is not necessarily black in another. People like the French novelist Alexandre Dumas and the Russian poet Aleksander Sergeevich Pushkin were considered white in Europe, but they identified themselves as black. And they would have been considered black in the United States because of the American definition of black as anyone with any black ancestry whatsoever. Pushkin's grandfather had been taken as a slave from Africa to Russia; Dumas' black mother was born in the West Indies. No wonder the contemporary slogan "Black Is Beautiful" means so much to American black people! After years of hiding and feeling shame for their bodies and their social condition, years that pitted light skin against dark, black people were happy when they could begin to develop and share pride in their own collective blackness. During the 1960's, many a fair-skinned passer "converted" and identified himself as black.

THE EUROPEAN AND AMERICAN INDIAN CONNECTIONS

When Admiral Penn captured Jamaica for the British in 1655, Oliver Cromwell, then the Lord Protector of England, saw the possibility of supplying people for the settlement of Jamaica while ridding England of some of its "undesirable" population at the same time. Irish vagabonds, condemned persons, and poor prisoners were shipped to Jamaica during the following years. While the Irish were not the only Europeans to occupy Jamaica, records of the period indicate that they became a majority.

The ensuing years brought a good deal of inter-marrying, resulting in a large population of black Jamaicans with Irish names that many Jamaicans still bear—McKay, McKeon, Collins, O'Hare, McCormack, Kennedy, McDermott, Walsh, and Burke. Some of these black Irish, as they have been called, migrated to the United States. Black Americans with Irish names—or those who know that Irish names were once part of their family—may be able to trace their families back to midseventeenth century Jamaica and even to Ireland.

Another instance of black families long entrenched in a particular area is the Cape Verdean people of New Bedford, Massachusetts. During the nineteenth century, American whalers had employed sailors from the Azores islands off the coast of Africa, colonized by the Portuguese. When the whalers returned to New Bedford, many of the sailors went with them and settled in the area, later bringing their families there from the Azores. The population of Cape Verdeans, who were a mixture of African and Portuguese blood, grew into large communities. Today, the people there still tend to be clannish, many of them continuing to live in New Bedford, their American "capital."

The Latin *Maurus*, a poetic term for someone from North Africa, occurs in European languages as Moor, More, Mor, Mohr, Maure, Moro, Morian, Morien and many other forms, and the term "blackamoor" was long used to mean Negro. In any case, the Moors of Europe have influenced all the great historical cultures, even Scandinavia. Many existing black coats of arms in

Europe attest to the degree of black influence, for they usually depict black faces and include a name that was some derivative or variation of the word Moor. Black Americans today have links to these early Moorish people. In fact, many Americans, white or black, whose name is in the Moor family—such as Murray, Morris, Morel, Morelli, Moreel, Morrison, Moreau, etc.—can assume there's Moorish blood somewhere in their ancestry.

But while the ties are strong between some black Americans and Europe, they are difficult to trace. Families were often divided in the course of the slave trade, members being sent to different countries besides America—Central America, South America, Cuba, Haiti, Jamaica, and other West Indian islands. With the various language barriers, differing cultural backgrounds, and changes of names that often occurred, it is extremely difficult to make family connections. Anyone wanting to pursue this would have to get some background on his family, knowing that there is a Moorish tie somewhere. A few of the coats of arms might be helpful, but they are located in European museums and national libraries. It might also be necessary to find the names of slave ships in which ancestors were transported—in all, a difficult and dubious undertaking. I have included a detailed list of European sources, though, for those ready to take the plunge.

Intermarriage and intermixing between blacks and Indians was generally more widespread and freer than black/white miscegenation. But the attitudes toward blacks differed from tribe to tribe, ranging from open acceptance and free mixing to downright prejudice and hostility.

The Choctaw, Chickasaw, and Cherokee, for example, all tended to denounce any intermarriage between their people and blacks, just as strongly as certain other tribes like the Creeks and especially the Seminoles seemed to accept it. Their cousins the Creeks were lukewarm on the subject.

Whites, of course, took advantage of any such situations, using the South Carolinian tribes, for instance, to help them hunt down fugitive slaves. Some tribes, like the Cherokee, went so far as to mimick whites and become slaveowners themselves and to adopt "black codes."

Given the minority status of both blacks and Indians, such a common bond of friendship would seem natural enough. After all, as far as the whites were concerned, the red man was inferior, too. In many states, in fact, the first slaves were Indians who had been captured in battle or kidnapped from their villages. The whites were understandably unhappy when the Indians appeared unable to adapt to slavery, their frail bodies withering under the hardships that blacks took as a matter of course. Thus, as the number of kidnapped Africans steadily increased, Indians were gradually phased out as slavery fodder.

Never quite willing to admit defeat, some slaveholders tried to keep some Indian women in an attempt to cross-breed able-bodied workers. But, unlike the transplanted blacks, Indians were familiar with local geography and were usually able to escape fairly easily from their self-styled masters. However, some Indians did remain on the plantations, intermarried with blacks and were slowly absorbed into the growing black population. When blacks and Indians were held together as slaves, the treatment for both was the same.

In general, however, Indians and blacks tended to mix rather freely. Certainly social barriers between the two groups were usually less restrictive than those set up between blacks and whites. For this reason, many Indian villages became natural havens for free blacks and fugitive slaves during the seventeenth and eighteenth centuries. Some tribes even made it an unstated rule to spare blacks during pitched battle while killing every white they could. By the midnineteenth century most eastern tribes—what was left of them—were heavily admixed with blacks.

The Jackson Whites of New Jersey originated when Indians were still living in the lowlands along the Ramapo Mountains. The first race resulted from a union between the Indians and half breeds on one side, and on the other, from black laborers brought from the lower part of the county to work in the Ramapo region. According to one source, a man named Jackson was ordered to furnish women for the brothels of the British soldiers in New York City. Shiploads of prostitutes were sent over, but one vessel was lost at sea. In order to compensate for this loss, Jackson acquired a shipload of black women from the West Indies. Some of these women, both white and black, were quartered in a stockade in the Lispenard Meadows in New York. When the British evacuated New York City in 1783, the women were released. Three thousand women ran down to the pier, jumped into small boats, and crossed over to the New Jersey shore. Male fugitives—Tories, Hessians, and runaway black slaves—followed them into the Ramapo Mountains where they settled.

Most subsequent blacks were either freed slaves or their children, and many of the names today may be traced as identified with some of the old Dutch pioneers

of Orangetown, where the slaves in old times bore the
surnames of their masters.

The strongest available proof we have for the extent
of black–Indian intermarriage are a number of petitions
filed by whites—another way whites attempted to
deprive various Indian tribes of their lands and rights.
They contended that because of the extensive mixing
between the Indians and blacks, the tribes could no
longer be considered "pure." According to the Bureau of
American Ethnology, for example, not one of the
members of the Pamunkey nation was a full-blooded
Indian as the nineteenth century came to a close. In
1822, the Narragansett tribe had a total of 429 members—
twenty-two Negroes and all the rest mixed Indian/
blacks. The local tribes around Montauk Point, New
York, intermarried so extensively that their modern
descendants have largely Negro blood in their veins—
they're considered Indian in name only. Other groups
like the Croatans of North Carolina, the Moors of
Delaware, and the Meguelons of Tennessee had to
undergo such racial identity attacks.

Given this free mixing, one would think marriage
records the logical place to start a search. Unfortunately,
tracing the lineage of people with such a heritage is
more difficult than you'd think, especially if you lack
some solid information to start with and have no living
relatives to provide firsthand information. Marriage
among the tribesmen of any Indian nation was seldom
a legal matter, therefore it was often impossible to tell
if a black was wife or concubine. Additionally, many
Indian males could take on as many wives as they
wished, while a female could dissolve a marriage
whenever she felt the need.

Such practices are not conducive to simple answers

or cursory research. Indians, like black Africans, relied primarily on their own system of oral history; they left few written records behind. The only way to approach the problem from the Indian side is through the existing records of the Bureau of Indian Affairs. In order to make your task even possible, however, you must know the particular tribe. Otherwise, you'll be lost in a maze. The only other feasible avenue of research would be through the normal sources you've been using all along —church records, census data, etc.—in the hope that some mention of Indian background was made somewhere.

But if you have unearthed any hints that lead you to suspect an unknown white relative or even a complete family branch, don't hesitate to take advantage of the probably abundant records they've left behind. Further information should be readily available in the major sources discussed in Chapter Three.

Chapter Seven

BACK TO AFRICA

You've spent hours interviewing existing relatives, scoured reams of dusty records, wandered through obscure museum collections searching for a single telltale clue, perhaps even visited some ancient family homesites to fill in a particularly stubborn gap.

You've contended with lost records, bad memories, illiteracy, the firsthand horrors of slavery, name changes, passing, white relatives, and every other kind of left-handed obstacle history could create.

And you've made it. Slowly, despite every roadblock, your family tree has blossomed, its branches suddenly drooping with unsuspected ancestors and their sad, frightening, brave, ironic life stories.

Yet no matter how successful you've been, the chances are that the final step in the search—actually tracing an ancestor back to Africa—is one few of us will be able to make. Even with the information I've provided in the next two chapters, such a task requires even more sweat and an uncommon bit of luck. But then, you just might be able to do it!

The final leap from America back to the tribes of ancient Africa is actually a three-step research process, each step progressively more distant and hard to take:

First, find the specific point-of-entry to the United States—the actual harbor where the slave ship docked.

Second, find the slave ship itself and what other stops it made between Africa and America.

Third, find the specific area the ship sailed from and the tribe from which your ancestor was kidnapped.

Before you run off to check any maritime record you can find, you have to face a couple of hard truths. For one thing, many historians believe that less than 10 percent of the slaves ever taken from Africa arrived in the United States. Those that survived the perilous journey—and many didn't—*might* have wound up in

America, but more likely went to the West Indies,
Cuba, Jamaica, Brazil, other South American countries,
or even Europe. Moreover, even the ships that eventually
docked in the States probably first stopped in the West
Indies, selling a portion of their human cargo to buy
rum and other goods. Even before undergoing the
trauma of the auction block, families found that they
were often separated along the way—a family of five
might well have wound up in five different parts of the
globe.

Just to take the first step in your new journey, you
must already have a good storehouse of information. If
you've traced your family back to a specific area, check
the port nearest that area. It might not be the point of
entry, but it's the logical place to start. Any hints you
manage to dredge up about the year a relative arrived in
America are invaluable; so are clues to where he landed.
What you really need to find is any list showing which
slaves were sold to which masters. If a master's name
with which you're familiar pops up, take down
everything you can about him. While it may not be a
sure thing, it might mean that one of the slaves he
bought that day was your great-great grandfather.

The name of the ancestor is, of course, essential, but
any other snippets—tribal marks, brands, handicaps,
even a hint about the tribe to which he belonged—will
probably be needed. Other clues will have to be fitted
in to the puzzle before it becomes a certainty.

The harbors that accommodated the many slave ships
are approximately the same as those still in existence—
Newport, Rhode Island; New York, New York; Boston,
Massachusetts; Baltimore, Maryland; Roanoke, Virginia;
Philadelphia, Pennsylvania; and Savannah, Georgia.

Lists of slaves sold at each port would, of course, be
invaluable and aid you immensely. Unfortunately, such

lists simply don't exist anymore, unless they are part of the maritime records of the slave ships themselves.

If you've managed to locate the probable entry point, visit the local historical society and the state archives. If they don't have any information, try the National Archives and the Library of Congress.

Other American sources would be the Insurance Company of North America (which insured many of the American slave traders), long-established brokerage houses, and any good maritime museum, especially the Mariners Museum of Newport News, Virginia.

Unfortunately, you'll quickly discover that none of the record sources have any separate listings for slave ships. They could be included in maritime records, port records, or any number of other logical and illogical categories. The best thing you can do is just talk to someone in charge and let them know what you're looking for and what information you already have to go on. Find out anything you can about ships that arrived at that port during the time period you're interested in, including such vital clues as the flag under which it flew, the name of the captain, where it sailed from, and of course, the name of the ship. Many slave ships were often named the *Africa*, the *Ruby*, the *Martha*, or the *Mary Adeline*.

The newspapers which you used so extensively in all your previous work could still provide some valuable clues. For example, the following advertisement for the "sale" of white indentured servants was printed in the *Virginia Gazette*, March 3, 1768:

Just arrived, the Neptune, Captain Arbuckle, with one hundred and ten HEALTHY Servants, Men, Women and Boys, among Whom are MANY VALUABLE TRADESMEN, viz.: Tailors, Weavers,

Barbers, Blacksmiths, Carpenters and Joiners,
Shoemakers, a Stay Maker, Cooper, Cabinet
Maker, Bakers, Silversmiths, a Gold and Silver
Refiner, and many others.

The Sale will commence at Leedstown, on the
Rappahannoc, on Wednesday, the 9th of this instant
[March]. A reasonable Credit will be allowed on
giving approved Security to

Thomas Hodge.

If you are unable to determine the exact point of
entry, skip over it. Just prepare for a long slog through
records dealing with all the slave ships in a particular
time period.

Before the 1780's, of course, America was still a group
of colonies under British rule, so American ships were
actually British ships flying the British flag. Lloyd's of
London, one of the oldest and largest insurance
companies of Great Britain, insured many of these early
slave ships. They even published a company newspaper,
the *Lloyd's List*, which charted the movements of its
vessels from the period of 1740 to 1826.

Here is an example of information on a ship in the
Lloyd's List for Tuesday, January 8, 1760:

The *Africa*, [captained by] Robe is arriv'd at
Carolina from Bonny [at the mouth of Niger's
Bonny River]; she came off the [slave] coast the
28th of June, and left the *Nancy*, of Bristol, who
was almost saved.

The list gives scanty information on each ship, but
slaves are occasionally mentioned in the brief reports.
The list does *not* include information on ships flying the
flags of France, Spain, or Portugal.

The records of the British Admiralty, the government

department with authority over all national naval affairs, include a lot of information on the papers dealing with the struggle in Britain to abolish the slave trade during the early nineteenth century.

Records of the British Museum and the House of Lords also include information which might prove helpful to some of you, though much of it pertains to the debates over abolition.

The slave trade *was* actually abolished in America in 1808—the *Clotilde* became the last *official* slave ship to reach our shores. (Cud-Joe-Lewis, a member of its cargo, became the last *official* slave to arrive in this country. Today his statue stands in front of the modest church he helped build in "Affriky-Town"—now Plateau—Alabama.

I've emphasized the word "official" because the slave trade *did* continue after 1808, even though it was a crime to participate in it. The profit potential was simply too large to be ignored, so a number of slave captains never gave up their livelihood.

While it was not extremely difficult to circumvent the new regulations, the captain usually had to bribe port officials to gain entry. And not all of them did—a surprising number were captured (and were often released by juries prone to turn a blind eye to such shenanigans). The logs of many of these ships still exist in either the National Archives or the Library of Congress, along with any other records about the specific ship that was confiscated. The log, if it is still preserved, could be invaluable, since it was a daily journal of everything that occurred on board during the voyage from Africa.

If you have no luck with American and British slave-ship records, the only recourse is probably the records

still in the West Indies, where many of the ships docked.
These records, unfortunately, are far from complete,
but a full list of sources in Jamaica, Haiti, and the other
Caribbean countries is included in the Appendix. It
would probably be foolish to schedule a trip to any of
these institutions without a pretty good idea of exactly
what you're looking for. Even then, a letter would be
far cheaper and probably accomplish the same thing.

Despite all these sources, don't be discouraged if
you're unable to get even a vague hint concerning any
slave ships. There's still a chance that you can get a very
good idea of where in Africa your family came from.

I got just such a hint some years ago, from a highly
unlikely source. While I was still in the armed forces, I
was walking down a street in Tokyo when two black
servicemen stopped me. One of them smiled and said,
"I bet I can tell you what part of Africa you come
from."

I was a little taken aback—here was a man I had
never seen before who claimed to know my origins! But
being interested in what he had to say, I listened.
"You," he proclaimed without any hesitation, "are from
Dahomey."

Before he entered the service, this man had studied
African features at the University of Minnesota. He said
it was often possible to tell what part of Africa an
individual was from just by studying the bone structure
of his face.

Well, I thought, that was a marvelous story. But I
didn't really believe it. Some years after that meeting in
Tokyo, however, I was discussing collections of rare
Afro-American literature before the American
Foundation for Negro Affairs in Philadelphia. Important
African scholars attended from all over the country.

During one of the workshops, a young man in the audience asked two Yale professors of African culture if they could identify the background of someone in the room just by his facial features. Both pointed to me almost immediately and said that, because of my physical features, my ancestors were probably from either Dahomey or Upper Volta.

Once could be coincidence, but twice makes you think. After the second incident, I started reading about Dahomey. When I visited Haiti, I learned that many Haitians actually originated in the Dahomey and Upper Volta area. Many aspects of Haitian culture, especially voodoo, were common in Dahomey as well. It seemed I had stumbled on an interesting method of identifying the original African tribal heritage of many blacks.

What makes this form of searching far easier is that some tribes were considered better "merchandise" than others—and were therefore shipped in disproportionate numbers. According to historian Carter G. Woodson:

> Slaves came in the main from Guinea and the Gold Coast, and Senegal. The Mandingoes were considered gentle in demeanor but prone to theft. The Coromantees brought from the Gold Coast were hearty and stalwart in mind and body, and for that reason frequently they were the source of slave insurrections which became the eternal dread of the masters. It was said, however, that the Coromantees were not revengeful when well treated. Slavers brought over some Whydahs, Nagoes and Pawpaws, as they were much desired by the planters because they were lusty, industrious, cheerful and sub- missive. There came also the Gaboons, who were physically weak and consequently unsuited for purposes of exploitation. The colonists imported, too, some Gambia Negroes, prized for their

meakness, whereas the Eboes from Calabar were not
desired, because they were proud and inclined to
commit suicide rather than bear the yoke of slavery.
The Congoes, Angolas, and the Eboes gave their
masters much trouble by running away. The Bantus
were also very proud and militant and fought back
European invasion.

As in the case of Haiti, certain sections of the United
States became settled with blacks from one or two
principal African regions. The Gullah people of South
Carolina—also known as the Sea Island people—have
long been of interest to folklorists and historians, many
of whom believe that they descended from the Angolan
and Yoruba peoples of West Africa.

Charlotte Forten, granddaughter of the famous
Revolutionary era black abolitionist James Forten, went
to South Carolina under the auspices of the Freedmen's
Bureau to help educate the Gullah people. Her diary
gives an excellent account of her stay there. The Gullahs
have lived on the South Carolina Sea Islands since the
time of slavery. Because they have been quite isolated
from the rest of the world, they have developed their
own dialect—a mixture of seventeenth and eighteenth
century English and various African languages. Today
many of the younger people are highly educated, living
and working in Savannah, Charleston, and other cities.
With the islands now being redeveloped, the displace-
ment of the Gullah people is inevitable. Anyone wishing
to do genealogical research in that area cannot afford to
delay.

Many modern Africans still seem to have this ability
to discern tribal ancestry from facial features alone.
Take advantage of it. Visit a nearby port where ships
from Africa frequently dock. If you have any notion

about the specific country your ancestors are from, try to find a ship from that country. Then talk to the sailors on board and see if they can identify what tribe your ancestor belonged to. It might help to bring along some photographs of other family members—the older the better—to give them more to work with. African students studying at American universities, members of embassies, consulates or other African officials might also be able to assist you in this simple method of tribal identification.

This method will not always work, especially since miscegenation with whites and Indians has blurred many of our original racial features. The less evidence of miscegenation in your family, the easier it will be to compare your features with those of existing nations and tribes. Even a consensus opinion could send you searching for books on Guinea or Dahomey, as it did me. You mightn't be able to trace your ancestors farther back, but you'll be able to learn a lot more about the country of your "birth."

Of course, a handful of you will not need such hints —you've actually managed to find the ship which brought an ancestor to America! For you, it's time for that final step—the trip back to Africa itself.

Chapter Eight

OUR AFRICAN HERITAGE

The eighteenth century witnessed a degree of black pride in the African heritage, as manifested in the names given to churches, fraternal organizations, and community groups—for example, the Free African Society, the African Mutual Aid Society, the African Marine Fund. But already Africa was strongly associated with the concepts of "primitive" and "pagan." The erudite but short-sighted philosophers we met in Chapter Four merely encouraged blacks to disparage their original homeland.

The poet Phillis Wheatley, born in Senegal around 1753 and sold into slavery in America as a young child, recorded these feelings in a poem entitled "On Being Brought from Africa to America."

> *Twas mercy brought me from my Pagan land,*
> *Taught me benighted soul to understand*
> *That there's a God, that there's a Savior too;*
> *Once redemption I neither sought nor knew,*
> *Some view our sable race with scornful eye,*
> *"Their color is a diabolic die."*
> *Remember, Christians, Negroes, black as Cain,*
> *May be refined, and join th'angelic train.*

While Harlem Renaissance writer Countee Cullen seemed to have a desire to venerate Africa, his 1925 poem "Heritage" reflects his ambivalence:

> *Africa? A book one thumbs*
> *Listlessly, till slumber comes.*

With such an outlook, cultural and genealogical ties with Africa were more likely to be denied than confirmed. It is only in recent years that some black Americans have been willing to point with pride rather than shame to their African heritage.

And indeed, there is certainly nothing to be ashamed of in our African heritage—because the picture of Africa that had been sold to our ancestors was false.

Dr. L. S. B. Leakey, in his book *The Progress and Evolution of Man in Africa*, states:

> In every country that one visits and where one is drawn into a conversation about Africa, the question is regularly asked, by people who should know better: 'But what has Africa contributed to world progress?' The critics of Africa forget that men of science today, with few exceptions, are satisified that Africa was the birthplace of man himself, and that for many hundreds of centuries thereafter, Africa was in the forefront of all human progress.

John W. Weatherwax, in his pamphlet, *The African Contribution*, tells us that Africans started mankind along the tool-making path—that skill which differentiates men from all other creatures. In his 1789 book, *Ruins of Empire*, Count C. F. Volney observed that:

> A people now forgotten [the black Egyptians] discovered, while others were yet barbarians, the elements of the arts and sciences. A race of men now rejected for their sable skin and frizzled hair founded on the study of the laws of nature, those civil and religious systems which still govern the universe. . . .

Africa has experienced three Golden Ages, two of which had reached their glory and were in decline while Europe was still a wilderness. The apex of Africa's first golden Age was Egypt from the Third Dynasty (c. 2600 B.C.) to the Twelfth Dynasty, when it was invaded by the Hyksos, or Shepherd Kings, c. 1700 B.C.

Imhotep, who lived during the 2700's B.C. and built the famous step pyramid of Saqqara, was one of the most outstanding personalities of Ancient Egypt. The methods he used revolutionized the tomb architecture of the ancient world. But Imhotep was more than just an architect—Sir William Osler in his book, *Evolution of Modern Medicine*, refers to him as "the first figure of a physician to stand out clearly from the mists of antiquity."

The Intermediate Period lasted about 185 years. Pharaoh Ahmose finally drove out the invaders, and Egypt's Eighteenth Dynasty was established, ushering in the nation's second Golden Age. Other nations to the south, Kush and Ethiopia, were part of this Golden Age and were contributors to the early culture of Egypt.

Queen Hatshepsut and her brother Thutmore III are well-known rulers of this period. They built great temples employing hundreds of artists and craftsmen. The artistic glories of Egypt were without equal. In 1370 B.C. Akenaton came to the throne and abandoned the many gods of Egyptian religion in favor of a single deity, the sun. He was the first temporal ruler to lead his people in worshipping one god.

After the Nineteenth Dynasty, Egypt's military and economic strength declined as wars of conquest and colonization took their toll. Kush or Ethiopia became more powerful. Makeda, the ruler of this empire around 900 B.C., is better known to the world as the Queen of Sheba. It is recorded that Makeda and King Solomon had a beautiful love affair that resulted in the birth of a son, Menelik. (Former Emperor Haile Selassie of modern Ethiopia descended from this lineage.) Ethiopia conquered Egypt, but though Egypt had become a colony, the Ethiopians founded its 24th dynasty and Egypt again became a world power.

By 671 B.C., the Assyrians drove out the Kushite
forces and destroyed Egypt's grandeur. As Egypt
declined, a new people, the Greeks, began to rise.
Then in 332 B.C. Alexander the Great invaded Egypt
—the first purely European invasion of Africa.

Joseph B. Danquah, a Ghanaian historian, states:

> By the time Alexander the Great was sweeping the
> civilized world with conquest after conquest from
> Chaeronia to Gaza, from Babylon to Cabril; by the
> time this first of the Aryan conquerors was learning
> the rudiments of war and government at the feet of
> philosophic Aristotle; and by the time Athens was
> laying down the foundations of modern European
> civilization, the earliest and greatest Ethiopian
> culture had already flourished and dominated the
> civilized world for over four and a half centuries.
> Imperial Ethiopia had conquered Egypt and founded
> the 25th Dynasty, and for a century and a half the
> central seat of civilization in the known world was
> held by the ancestors of the modern Negro, main-
> taining and defending it against the Assyrians and
> Persian Empire of the East.
>
> Thus, at the time when Ethiopia was leading the
> civilized world in culture and conquest, East was
> East but West was as yet to be held. Rome was
> nowhere to be seen on the map, and sixteen
> centuries were to pass before Charlemagne would
> rule in Europe and Egbert become the first king of
> England.

North Africa was Rome's bread basket, hence the
Punic Wars between Rome and Carthage and the
Roman invasion of Egypt during Cleopatra's reign. In
the seventh century A.D., Arabs conquered this part of
the world and established an empire from the Pyrenees
to the Bosporus.

In Southern Rhodesia lie the famed ruins of Zimbabwe, a complex of 30-foot walls, turrets, and chambers built entirely of fitted stones without any mortar whatsoever! When the site was first discovered in 1868, white explorers refused to consider that such inspired stonework could have been the work of blacks, but much of the ornamental stonework bears inescapably African motifs. Recent carbon-dating of wood fragments found at the site indicate that Zimbabwe was occupied as late as A.D. 600, but the ruins themselves may well be older still.

The Benin nation in southern Nigeria was still a thriving metropolis when European traders first arrived. Although the Bini people had developed no written language, they had evolved a sophisticated currency system based on cowrie shells and *manillas*, or small metal rings. The Bini merchants stocked ironwork, fresh and preserved foodstuffs, tools, weaponry and artwork, and were expert negotiators. "We generally have to wait eight or ten days," one early white traveler complained, "before we can agree upon a price."

The tribal wars encouraged by the slave trade eventually led to Benin's collapse, and in 1897, when British troops marched in to seize the capital, the nation ceased to exist. But the civilization lives on in its renowned sculptures and bas-reliefs that the *Oba*, or King of Benin, used to decorate his palace beginning in about the thirteenth century. These bronze artworks, as sophisticated as the best statues of Greece or Rome, show a breathtaking record of Benin's glory—warriors, royalty, court attendants, acrobats, musicians, and hunters are depicted as they were in life. And when these pieces come on the art market—as they do, infrequently—they command prices that equal those paid for Impressionist paintings.

The last Golden Age of Africa occurred in that part of West Africa known as the Western Sudan. In Ghana an ancient culture was established in the third century A.D. By A.D. 1062, Ghana had reached the pinnacle of its greatness and was the commercial center of western Africa. Its empire was highly organized, and its standard of living high.

In the eleventh century, the Almoravides, a Berber people, conquered Ghana in a *jihad*, or holy war, thus ending Ghana's eight-hundred-year history of prosperity and cultural development. Although the Empire of Ghana regained its independence in 1087, it remained weak and became a part of the Mali Empire.

Mansa Musa, who reigned in the fourteenth century, was the most famous emperor of the Mali Empire. Timbuktu (or Tombouctou) was the major city and competed with the city of Gao, jewel of the Songhai Empire, two hundred miles down the Niger River. When Mansa Musa visited Timbuktu in 1324 enroute to Mecca he supposedly had an entourage of sixty thousand persons. Five hundred servants preceded the emperor, each of them carrying a staff of pure gold. Over 2,400 pounds of gold were distributed as alms. On his return from Mecca, Musa brought with him an architect who designed a number of beautiful buildings throughout his realm. Musa conquered the Songhai Empire and rebuilt the University of Sankoré in Timbuktu, but after his death the Empire of Mali declined. Songhai came back into its own.

The greatest king of the Songhai Empire was Muhammad Askia the Great, also known as Muhammad Toure, who came to power in 1493. His empire was eventually larger than the entire European continent. In his famous book, *Travels and Discoveries in North and Central Africa,* the German writer Henry Barth called him "one of the most brilliant and enlightened administrators of all times." And Alexander Chamberlain, in his book, *The Contribution of the Negro to Human Civilization*, wrote:

> In personal character, in administrative ability, in devotion to the welfare of his subjects, in open-mindedness toward foreign influences and in wisdom in the adoption of enlightened ideas and institutions from abroad, King Askia was certainly the equal of the average European monarch of the time and superior to many of them.

Under Askia's leadership the realm became famous for its intellectual centers, wealth, and "dazzling women." The University of Sankoré in Timbuktu hosted scholars from around the world. According to Leo Africanus, "In Timbuktu there are numerous judges, doctors and clerks, all receiving good salaries from the king. He pays great respect to men of learning. There is a big demand for books in manuscript, imported from Barbary [North Africa]. More profit is made from the book trade than from any other line of business."

The culture that Africanus pictured has been beautifully summed up by Roi Ottley in *No Green Pastures:*

> The city's universities and libraries were famous, and the manufacture and sale of books was one of the important businesses.
> African blacks astounded the most learned men of Islam by their erudition. These people were the first to smelt iron. They invented at least four different alphabets, with characters as phonetic symbols. There are today approximately six hundred languages and dialects among the blacks in Africa.

The richness and flexibility of these tongues is
reported to be such that each has twenty or more
words to describe a man walking, sauntering, or
swaggering. Thus the African is able to express the
most delicate shades of thought and sentiment. Built
on systematic and philosophic foundations, and
grammatical principles, few languages have such
breadth, character and precision.

After Askia died in 1538, the strong hold that he had
exerted over the vast territory weakened. In 1590 the
sultan of Morocco invaded the Songhay Empire with a
storehouse of European firearms. In the devastation that
ensued Timbuktu was plundered. And the University of
Sankoré, which had existed for over five hundred years,
was destroyed, its professors exiled to Morocco. Felix
Du Bois, in *Timbuctoo the Mysterious*, says:

Among the exiles was a learned doctor, Ahmed
Baba by name, born in 1556 at Arawan. In spite of
his youth, he enjoyed a considerable reputation in
Timbuctoo at the time of the Moorish conquest, and
his brethren gave him the title of "the Unique Pearl
of his Times." In the Bedzl of Morrasaka, one of the
ancient Moroccan histories, it is reported that
Ahmed said: "Of all my friends I had the fewest
books, and yet when your soldiers despoiled me
they took sixteen hundred volumes."

Ahmed was eventually given his liberty. He returned
to Timbuktu where he died in 1627, a man of great
erudition and a prolific writer. He is known to have
authored forty books, including commentaries on the
Koran, an astronomical treatise written in verse, and
others elucidating the law and the sciences he professed.
    The ruthless Moorish occupation destroyed the highly
civilized society it had taken hundreds of generations to

construct and decimated the population. The Moors
were slave hunters. They and the Europeans who
followed soon after were responsible for the eventual
trade in human beings which made possible the
development of the New World.

The greedy Europeans, witnessing the havoc that had
occurred in Africa, fully believed that this was the
continent's normal condition. Hence their rationalizations
for the inferiority of black people. But still, despite the
native wars and devastation, there remained highly
civilized black tribes whose virtues amazed white
travelers. In his autobiography, *A Slaver's Log Book*,
Captain Theophilus Conneau describes his 1827
encounter with the Bager people:

> On my arrival the oldest man of the town, who
> invariably acts as the Chief, welcomed me to his
> hut. Having made my declaration of the purpose of
> my visit, I demanded to be shown the house of my
> trader.
>
> The old patriarch took me to a distant dilapidated
> hut whose roof was supported by only four posts
> without walls. Here I recognized a large trade chest,
> a rum cask, and my trader's grass hammock. In
> wonder I demanded why my property was thus
> exposed.
>
> I was informed by my conductor that this was my
> trader's habitation, that my property being under
> the shade of the sun and rain, it was perfectly safe.
> I opened the chest, which to my still greater surprise
> I found unlocked. And lo, I saw it nearly full with
> the same goods I had filled it. Struck with amaze-
> ment, I again questioned the head man why my
> trader was not supplied with a better house, and my
> goods a safer place free from theft.
>
> The old gentleman answered with a gentle smile
> and said that they, the Bagers, were neither Sosoos

nor white men; that a stranger's property was as
safe as their own; that their labor supplied them
with food and all the necessities of life; that they
had no need to steal from their guests or to sell one
another. As I still doubted this never-to-be-forgotten
public and national honesty, my trade man led me
to a neighboring lemon tree and there showed me a
pair of English brass steelyards hanging on its
branches. He told me that they formerly belonged to
a Mulatto trader from Sierra Leone who had died in
the town on a trading trip, and that the steelyards
as well as a chest half full of goods had been kept
above 12 years in expectation that some of his
friends from the Colony would call for them. I
found that even when a poor Black stranger
demanded hospitality everyone in the town shared
in the charity.

I have never read an account of these worthy
Africans, which in honesty could be compared with
the most civilized nation of the world. Why then,
civilize this people and teach them Christian
selfishness!

A study of the various tribes in Africa is intriguing,
since although there are some similarities among the
people in terms of customs and physical characteristics,
there are also a great many dissimilarities. The Pygmies
of the Ituri rain forest are the world's shortest people,
while the Dinka of the upper Nile are among the
world's tallest. The tribes of the equatorial forests have
broad noses, and the Batusi have thin noses. The Belega
of Zaire have massive bone structures and well-developed
muscles. The Dinka, Batusi, Bahima, and Masai have
slender builds and long, thin legs.

Some groups who have lived in complete isolation
with no intermingling with other groups have developed

very distinguishing characteristics. The Khoisan group, which is composed of Hottentots and Bushmen, have yellow skin, gray hair, flat faces, and steatopygia— an accumulation of excessive fat on the buttocks, a common characteristic among Hottentot women.

Anthropologists used to think that there was a racial affinity between Khoisans and Asiatics. Now they believe that the Khoisans are just a special group of Africans. Similarly, some students have believed that the infusion of non-African blood resulted in the characteristics of the dark-skinned, tall, slender, narrow-nosed, thin faced Batusi of Rwanda and Burundi, the Bahima of Uganda, and the Masai in Kenya. The most recent anthropological data now view these characteristics as an evolutionary tendency native to black Africa.

Africa is a very large continent, and slaves were taken from all parts of it. But as we've seen, most slaves were brought to the New World from West Africa. To find which country or nation your ancestor came from will be no small feat, but the first step—locating the general area—is actually easy now. Because even if you don't have enough clues by now, there's just no place else to look!

Before you give up entirely, go over *all* the information you've collected. Search for anything that even hints at a specific area or nation. After you've ascertained the specific area or country from which your ancestor was most likely kidnapped, the final step is to find the exact tribe. A few of the most likely are listed below.

The **Guro** (or Kweni) people, who live in the interior of the Ivory Coast, were heavily depopulated by the slave trade. The Guro are of Mande (or Mandingo) origin. Half of their villages are in the forest and the other half located in the savanna. They have no chiefs of any sort—a council of elders resolves all disputes at the family, village, and tribal level.

A Guro can never become too rich. He becomes rich by hunting, weaving, agriculture, commerce, forging iron, or war and must therefore control a large number of dependents, either relatives or clients. He is then given the title "migone." But now he is expected to be very generous, and when he dies, the cost of the lavish funeral, befitting his stature in the community, reduces his family to poverty again! This system ensures the egalitarian character of the society without taking away individual initiative.

The **Hausa** people live in the northwestern part of Nigeria and the eastern part of Niger. The people resemble the Sudanese, but their language has a close affinity to the Hamitic-Semitic group of languages.

The travelers Ibu Battuta and Leo Africanus wrote about the Hausa and their lands as far back as the fourteenth century. Their economy has been one of the most developed in Africa since the Middle Ages. Good farmers and herdsmen and expert urban craftsmen, they also developed leatherwork and weaving to a high art form. The work of the craftsmen resulted in widespread trade with commercial enterprises, in association with the Mandingo people.

Muslims first made contact with the Hausa in the fourteenth century when they were under the influence of Mali. A *jihad* was waged against the Hausa in the nineteenth century by the Fulani religious leader, Usuman Dan Fodio. After a century of power, the Empire of Sokoto was destroyed by European colonization. The descendents of the Hausa, who had been exported as slaves, played an important role in the events which led to the slave uprisings in Brazil and Jamaica in the nineteenth century.

Today the Hausa are still keen merchants. To show how active their trading has been, today the Hausa language is spoken by many ethnic groups. In Cameroun, the word "Hausa" has become another word for "Muslim peddler," no matter what the merchant's heritage.

Many black Americans can trace their ancestry from the **Ibo** tribe. There are still about 8 million Ibos in the eastern section of Nigeria, but the slave trade took a heavy toll of their population.

Perhaps more than other tribes, the Ibos cherish individualism—their society is characterized by democracy, religious sanctions and the glorification of personal success. Even today, the Ibo are prominent in Nigeria's political and economic life.

The **Senufo** tribe, another people inhabiting the West Coast of Africa, came from the territory further north about three centuries ago. They number about 1 million people and live in the area divided by the Ivory Coast, Mali, and Upper Volta. They keep to themselves, showing no interest in the outside world, and usually marry within the same village. Sometimes a wife will continue to live with her own people, and her husband will come to visit her two or three times a week. The children of such a union belong to the mother's lineage.

There is a village chief and also someone who is called a "master of the land." This person is a representative of the first inhabitants, and he serves as a priest, mediating between the seen and unseen worlds. The Senufo do not regard the earth as something that can be owned, but as a divinity.

The **Yoruba** people live in southwestern Nigeria and in southeastern and central Dahomey. They are about 8 million in number. Yorubaland was one of the greatest art centers in the whole of Africa. Religion, court, and popular art existed side by side. The Yorubas were so artistic that they even carved the wooden doors to their homes with scenes depicting everyday life, history, or myth.

Speaking of myth, the Yorubas have one of the richest mythologies in West Africa. They have 201 gods who maintain a continuity through the ancestors. This mythology and form of worship, brought to the West Indies and Brazil by slaves bought off the coast of Nigeria, Dahomey, and Togo, is known as voodoo, which is derived from the Fon word *vodu*. The corresponding Yoruba word is *orisha*. Fon is the language of the Dahomey, and Yoruba is spoken in Nigeria and parts of Dahomey. Voodoo is a highly complex system of religious ideas that varies from one region to another. However, Shango, the god of thunder, is as much alive in Haiti and Brazil as he is on the West Coast of Africa.

Many tribes of three or four centuries ago just aren't around today, either destroyed or fully assimilated by the colonial powers. But of course there's still that one chance you've been fighting for all along. If you are ever to find out this information with any certainty, a trip to Africa will most likely be necessary.

If you are determined to make that trip, send off letters of credentials to those from whom you seek assistance. Write to the American embassy, the universities, African friends living in the area, and any appropriate government agency. Let the United Nations missions and embassies in this country help you in learning about the country and guiding you to its resources. After arriving in Africa, you can consult with archivists and historians there.

AFRICAN SOCIETY

Once you know where you come from, it becomes relatively easy to reestablish your family tree on African soil. One reason is the high regard Africans place in kinship. Indeed, ancestor worship is a natural "religion" common to all African tribes. Ancestors represent the source of life and prosperity and therefore appear often in the art of the African—in masks, statues, and figurines. Their memory is forever in the hearts, minds, and souls of their descendents, receiving daily offerings and invocations from the family.

In their art, the Africans show their belief that the ancestors were strong and full of vitality. The Primal Ancestor is not regarded as being male or female and is portrayed as nude, although adult nudity in real life is rare. Though the rest of the statue is an abstraction, the genitals are carved realistically, symbolizing the fecundity of the Ancestor and not lust. The clan strength, the importance of the principle of descent, and the values of virility expressed in the statues of the ancestors are also detected in the worship rites performed for the Ancestor, quite real to his descendents. African life would be hard if not impossible without the solidarity of the family tree.

A clan in African society, similar to the village unit, is based entirely on kinship, not on land ownership. The authorities of a clan wield power because they are descended from a particular ancestor. People know they belong to the same clan if they recognize the same ancestor and are bound by the same taboos and rituals.

A tribe is similar to a clan, but on a larger basis. Originally, tribes were just groups who thought themselves descended from the same ancestor. They developed a society in which the group as a whole and the individual

could develop harmoniously. Even today, members of
the same tribe share the same philosophy, speak the same
language, and follow the same customs.

African children learn the rights and obligations that
they will have to assume during their lifetime, such as the
relationship between a brother and an older brother or a
daughter and her mother. In some societies in Africa,
relations of a certain age or generation and sex are called
by the same term. Thus a child may have several
"mothers" or "fathers," "uncles" or "brothers." There are
usually many types of groups within the tribe. Membership in some groups means that an individual is never
alone; misfortunes, fortunes, hostility, and the trials of
everyday living are absorbed by a community of
"brothers" who assist and protect each other.

One tribe may trace its kinship or lineage from the
male side—known as patrilineage—and another tribe
may trace its lineage from the female side—known as
matrilineage. Such kinship systems have been very
important in African life. These bonds of kinship define
an individual's profession, class, education, etc., and
dictate how one individual will relate to another.

Most African tribes have secret societies—some
beneficial and others set up to keep the population in
line with fear, such as the Lo institution of the Senufos.
Only males are allowed in the organization. Esoteric
information is kept from women. There are three stages
in the Lo organization, each of which lasts seven years.
The first stage covers childhood, the second adolescence,
and the third adult life. Special rites of initiation mark the
passage from one stage to another. A young man must
pass all the trials before becoming a member of the
organization and must be thirty years old before he can
enter the final stage. Once the man is initiated, however,

he is considered an elder and is no longer required to perform agricultural tasks. The chief consults the elders before making any important decisions.

Such an elder may even be able to locate a *griot* whose main function in life is to recount orally the history of a specific village or clan. The word *griot* is probably a corruption of the Wolof word *gewel* or the Portuguese word *criado*. The griots were a professional group found among the Wolof, Serer, Fulani, Mande, Songhai, and other peoples of the West Coast, functioning as story-tellers, heralds, genealogists, musicians, oral reporters, or paid flatterers.

A griot could be male or female. Some had special family names; others took the name of some noble clan. They lived at the courts of the chiefs or in their own special place in the village. Some of them became extremely powerful and served as advisers to the chief or held other positions of political importance. They were often both feared and despised.

Today, many griots work at other more modern professions, such as teaching college, serving as priests, even factory work. Some societies, like the Bantu-speaking peoples of the East African lakes region, still hold the griot in a position of honor. But in some West African societies, the griot is discriminated against, usually on the excuse that his or her ancestor broke one of the society's major taboos.

But despite their assimilation into modern African society, if you are lucky enough to find a griot from your original tribe, as Alex Haley did, your search is over. You'll be able to sit at the feet of this living history book and learn everything about your family from centuries ago.

Another important source in your search might be the American Colonization Society. Formed in 1816 by a

group of distinguished white Americans, such as "Star
Spangled Banner" author Francis Scott Key, its goal was
to establish a colony for free blacks in Liberia and Sierra
Leone. Despite the strong opposition of Frederick
Douglass and other eminent blacks, it was strongly
supported by the slave holders who weren't comfortable
with American blacks having free status, and the group
successfully returned many blacks to African colonies.

When the American blacks founded Liberia, most of
them made their home in Monrovia, the capital of
Africa's first independent black nation. Monrovia is still
the capital today. The American blacks known as the
Amerigo-Liberians became the rulers and an aristocracy
of sorts because of their superior education.

For years, the American Colonization Society published
its *Proceedings*, which give detailed information about
the African colonies—invaluable sources for people who
have learned that their ancestors returned to Liberia or
Sierra Leone. For copies, check the Library of Congress
and the National Archives.

For tracing families to Liberia, there is an excellent
source—a rare pamphlet in the National Archives that
gives the census report of black immigrants to Liberia.
Printed in Washington, D.C. in 1845, it is entitled *Table
Showing the Number of Immigrants and Recaptured
Africans Sent to the Colony of Liberia by the Government
of the United States. Also the Number Who Purchased
Freedom, The Number Emancipated, and etc. Together
With a Census of the Colony and a Report of its
Commerce, etc. September 1843.*

The papers of Yehudi Ashumn, a scholar connected
with the society, might also provide important information. As far as I know, they are either in the Archives or
Library of Congress. Ask the people you've dealt with at
each to help you locate them.

The capital of Sierra Leone was Freetown, where many blacks from Nova Scotia wound up. Some of these were Maroons from Jamaica, slaves who had fought the British. The archives in Sierra Leone would be a good source for seeking information concerning their migration. Also check the files of the Christian missionaries, who kept their excellent records in Freetown and the British Museum.

For better or worse, you've come to the end of a long journey. You may have stayed with us to the end or dropped out along the way, but it is hoped that you have discovered some fascinating details about your families and, consequently, learned something about your own life as well. And maybe you've gotten a sense of pride too, knowing how great Africa once was, and consequently, how great *we* can be. If you have been touched along the way, then the hours of searching have been well worth it. For all of us.

Appendix A

DIRECTORY OF RESEARCH SOURCES

Note:

An asterisk (*) after the date indicates that that is the time the state started to record the statistics.

Inquiries to any Federal Archives and Records Center should be addressed to "Chief, Archives Branch."

Individuals to be contacted are listed following the address of the library or organization.

ALABAMA

Alabama Department of Archives and History
624 Washington Avenue
Montgomery, AL 36104

Alabama Historical Association
3121 Carlisle Road
Birmingham, AL 35213

Alabama Public Library Service
155 Administration Building
Montgomery, AL 36104
Anthony Miele, Director
Telephone: (205) 832-5743

Bureau of Vital Statistics
State Department of Public Health
Montgomery, AL 36104
(Births and deaths 1908.* Marriages August 1936.* Marriage records can also be found in the probate court of each county.)

Mobile County Board of Health
P. O. Box 4533
Mobile, AL 36604
(Births 1871,* deaths 1820.*)

Historic Mobile Preservation Society
350 Oakleigh Place
Mobile, AL 36604

Southern Society of Genealogists (SSG)
Stewart University
Centre, AL 35960
Mrs. Frank Ross Stewart, Executive Director
(Membership of fifty professional genealogists. Encourages
genealogical research, conducts seminars, publishes annual
directory.)

Tuskegee Institute
Washington Collection
Hollis Burke Frissell Library
Tuskegee, AL 36088

ALASKA

Bureau of Vital Statistics
State Department of Health and Welfare
State Office Building
Juneau, AK 99801
(Records 1913.*)

Department of Education
Pouch G
State Capitol Building
Juneau, AK 99801
Richard Engen, Director of Libraries
Telephone: (907) 586-5242

AMERICAN SAMOA

Government of American Samoa
Pago Pago, American Samoa 96920
Registrar of Vital Statistics
(Births, deaths, marriages 1909.*)

ARIZONA

Arizona Historical Foundation
Hayden Memorial Library
Arizona State University
Tempe, AZ 85281

Arizona Historical Society
949 E. 2nd Street
Tucson, AZ 85719

Arizona State Department of Library and Archives
3rd Floor, State Capitol
Phoenix, AZ 85007

Bureau of Vital Statistics
State Board of Health
Phoenix, AZ 85007

Department of Administration
Division of Library Archives and Public Records
Phoenix, AZ 85007
Marguerite B. Cooley, Assistant Director
Telephone: (602) 271-5101

ARKANSAS

Arkansas Historical Association
History Department
University of Arkansas
Fayetteville, AR 72703

Arkansas Historical Commission
300 W. Markham Street
Little Rock, AR 72201

Arkansas Library Commission
506½ Center Street
Little Rock, AR 72201
Karl Neal, Executive Secretary
Telephone: (501) 371-1524

Bureau of Vital Statistics
State Department of Health
4815 W. Markham Street
Little Rock, AR 72201
(Births and deaths 1914,* marriages 1917.*)

Philander Smith College Library
812 W. 13th Street
Little Rock, AR 72202

BAHAMAS

Bahamas Historical Society
Nassau, New Providence, Bahamas

Archives Section
Ministry of Education and Culture
P. O. Box N3913
Nassau, New Providence, Bahamas

CALIFORNIA

Bureau of Vital Statistics and Data Processing
State Department of Public Health
631 J Street
Sacramento, CA 95814
(Births and deaths 1905.* Marriage records are kept by county clerks,
July 1905.*)

Alameda County Health Department
499 5th Street
Oakland, CA 94607

Berkeley City Health Department
Bureau of Vital Statistics
2121 McKinley Avenue
Berkeley, CA 94703

Vital Statistics Office
Long Beach City Health Department
P. O. Box 6157
Long Beach, CA 90806

Los Angeles County Health Department
Room 900
220 N. Broadway
Los Angeles, CA 90012

Pasadena City Health Department
Division of Vital Statistics
100 N. Garfield Avenue
Pasadena, CA 91109

San Francisco Department of Public Health
101 Grove Street
San Francisco, CA 94102

California Department of Parks and Recreation
P. O. Box 2390
Sacramento, CA 95811

California Historical Society
2090 Jackson Street
San Francisco, CA 94115

California State Archives
1020 O Street
Sacramento, CA 95814

California State Library
P. O. Box 2037
Sacramento, CA 95809
Ethel H. Crocket, State Librarian
Telephone: (916) 445-2585 or 445-4027

Federal Archives and Records Center
1000 Commodore Drive
San Bruno, CA 94066
Telephone: (415) 876-9001
(Serves northern California, Hawaii, Nevada [except Clark County],
and the Pacific Ocean area.)

Federal Archives and Records Center
24000 Avila Road
Laguna Miguel, CA 92677
Telephone: (714) 831-4220
(Serves Arizona, the southern California counties of Imperial, Inyo,
Kern, Los Angeles, Orange, Riverside, San Bernardino, San Diego,

San Luis Obispo, Santa Barbara, and Ventura, and Clark County,
Nevada.)

Henry E. Huntingdon Library and Art Gallery
1151 Oxford Road
San Marino, CA 91108

Historical Society of Southern California
200 East Avenue, 43
Los Angeles, CA 90031

University of California at Berkeley
Center of Real Estate and Urban Economics Library
260 Stephens Memorial Hall
Berkeley, CA 94720

University of California at Berkeley
Survey Research Center
International Data Library and Reference Service
2220 Piedmont Avenue
Berkeley, CA 94720

University of California at Los Angeles
Institute of Government and Public Affairs
Social Sciences 11252
Los Angeles, CA 90024

University of California at Los Angeles
Library, Department of Special Collections
120 Powell Library
Los Angeles, CA 90024

University of California at Santa Barbara
Wyles Collection
Goleta, CA 93106

CANADA

London Public Library and Art Museum
London, Ontario

McMaster University Mills Memorial Library
Hamilton, Ontario

National Library
395 Wellington Street
Ottawa, Ontario

Public Archives of Nova Scotia
Coburg Road
Halifax, Nova Scotia

Toronto Public Library
Toronto, Ontario

University of King's College Library
Toronto, Ontario

CANAL ZONE

Canal Zone Government
Health Director's Office
Box M
Balboa Heights, C.Z.
Registrar of Vital Statistics
(Births and deaths 1905.*)

CENTRAL AFRICAN REPUBLIC

Office de la Recherche Scientifique et Technique
Outre-Mer Centre ORSTOM de Bangui
B. P. 893
Bangui, C. A. R.

Université Jean Bedel Bokassa
B. P. 1450
Bangui, C. A. R.

COLORADO

Colorado State Library
1362 Lincoln Street
Denver, CO 80203
Richard M. Cheski, Assistant Commissioner
Telephone: (303) 892-2174

Federal Archives and Records Center
Building 48, Denver Federal Center
Denver, CO 80225
Telephone: (303) 234-3187
(Also serves Montana, North Dakota, South Dakota, Utah, and
Wyoming.)

Records and Statistics Section
State Department of Health
4210 E. 11th Avenue
Denver, CO 80220
(Births and deaths 1910.* Some records date back to 1860's. Marriages
1904–1940 and 1968.*)

State Historical Society of Colorado
200 14th Avenue
Denver, CO 80203

PEOPLE'S REPUBLIC OF CONGO

Conseil National de la Recherche Scientifique et Technique
Brazzaville, P. R. C.

Bibliothèque de l'Université de Brazzaville
B. P. 2025
Brazzaville, P. R. C.

CONNECTICUT

Connecticut Historical Society
1 Elizabeth Street
Hartford, CT 06105

Connecticut State Library
231 Capitol Avenue
Hartford, CT 06115
Charles Funk, State Librarian
Telephone: (203) 566-4192

Norfolk Historical Society
Village Green
Norfolk, CT 06058

Public Health Statistics Section
State Department of Health
79 Elm Street
Hartford, CT 06115
(Births and deaths 1897.* Birth records strictly confidential. Birth,
death, and marriage records are also filed with each town clerk.)

Yale University
James Weldon Johnson Memorial Collection of Negro Arts and Letters
Sterling Memorial Library
1603A Yale Station
New Haven, CT 06520

CUBA

Academia de Ciencias de Cuba
Capitolio Nacional
Havana, Cuba

Biblioteca Central "Ruben Martinez Villena" de la Universidad
de la Habana
Havana, Cuba

Instituto de Historia
Compostela y San Isidro, Cuba

Instituto del Libro
Calle 19
Havana, Cuba

Museo de la Habana
Oficina del Historiador
Palacio de los Capitanes Generales
Plaza de Armas
Havana, Cuba

DAHOMEY

Archives Nationales de la République du Dahomey
B. P. No. 3
Porto Novo, Dahomey

Université du Dahomey
Abomey-Calavy
B. P. 526
Cotonou, Dahomey

DELAWARE

Bureau of Vital Statistics
State Board of Health
P. O. Box 637
Dover, DE 19901
(Births and deaths 1860,* marriages 1847.* For earlier records, check
with clerk of the peace in each county.)

Delaware Department of Historical and Cultural Affairs
Hall of Records
Dover, DE 19901

Delaware Public Archives Commission
Hall of Records
Dover, DE 19901

Delaware State College
William C. Jason Library
Dover, DE 19901

Department of Community Affairs and Economic Development
P. O. Box 635
Dover, DE 19901
Director, Division of Libraries
Telephone: (302) 678-4748

Historical Society of Delaware
505 Market Street
Wilmington, DE 19801

University of Delaware
Division of Urban Affairs
Newark, DE 19711

DISTRICT OF COLUMBIA

American Society of Genealogists (ASG) sponsors the Institute of Genealogical Research at American University, Washington, D.C. (Specialists in genealogy and heraldry have published *Genealogical Research: Methods and Sources.*)

Association of the Study of Afro American History
1538 9th Street, N.W.
Washington, D.C. 20009

District of Columbia Department of Public Health
Vital Records Division
300 Indiana Avenue, N.W.
Washington, D.C. 20001
(Births 1871,* deaths 1855.* Marriages 1811.*)

Marriage License Bureau
U.S. District Court
Washington, D.C.
(No death records filed during the Civil War.)

Howard University
Afro-American Collection
Founders Library
2401 6th Street N.W.
Washington, D.C. 20001

Martin Luther King Library
901 G Street, N.W.
Washington, D.C. 20001
Dr. Hardy R. Franklin, Director
Telephone: (202) 727-1111

National Genealogical Society (NGS)
1921 Sunderland Place, N.W.
Washington, D.C. 20036
Virginia Davis Westhaeffer, President
Telephone: (202) 785-2123
(Fosters genealogical interest—national, state, county, township, city

and town, church, cemetery, and Bible and family records. Members
can exchange data with others interested in the same families.
Maintains library of 10,000 volumes on genealogy, local history,
and source material.)

National Archives and Records Service
General Services Administration
8th and Pennsylvania Avenue, N.W.
Washington, D.C. 20408

National Society Daughters of the American Revolution
1776 D Street, N.W.
Washington, D.C. 20006
Mrs. Wakelee Rawson Smith, President General
Telephone: (202) 628-4980
(Society of women descendants of Revolutionary War patriots.
Maintains genealogical/historical research library, Americana
museum, and documentary collections antedating 1830.)

National Society Sons of the American Revolution
2412 Massachusetts Avenue, N.W.
Washington, D.C. 20008

ENGLAND

The British Library
Reference Division
Great Russell Street
London, England

Lloyd's of London
Lime Street
London EC3M 7HA, England

Public Record Office
Chancery Lane
London, England

Society of Genealogists
37 Harrington Gardens
S.W. 7 4JX
London, England
Mrs. C. M. Mackay, Secretary
(Encourages study and research in genealogy, heraldry, and topography. Maintains library of 30,000 volumes, over 4,000 parish register copies, a document collection arranged by family and place of 11,000 file boxes, card index of 3 million names, marriage index of 7 million names, and collections relating to professions, schools, universities, military services, inns of court, religions, peerage, heraldry, and English persons living abroad in the Commonwealth and in America. Publishes register of members, including genealogical interests.)

FLORIDA

Black Research Information Coordinating Services, Inc.
614 Howard Avenue
Tallahassee, FL 32304

Bureau of Vital Statistics
State Department of Health
P. O. Box 210
Jacksonville, FL 32201
(Births 1865,* deaths 1877,* marriages 1927.* Write to county judge in each county for marriage records.)

Division of Library Services
Department of State
Tallahassee, FL 32301
Cecil P. Beach, Director
Telephone: (904) 488-2088

Florida Division of Archives, History, and Records Management
401 E. Gaines Street
Tallahassee, FL 32301

Historical Association of Southern Florida
3290 S. Miami Avenue
Miami, FL 33129

St. Augustine Historical Society
271 Charlotte Street
St. Augustine, FL 32084

FRANCE

Archives Nationales
60 Rue des Francs-Bourgeois
Paris, France

Bibliothèque de l'Institut National des Langues et Civilisations
    Orientales
2 Rue de Lille
Paris, France

Bibliothèque Nationale
58 Rue de Richelieu
Paris, France

Bibliothèques des Universités de Paris (one part of that consortium of
    libraries)
Bibliothèque de Documentation Internationale Contemporaine
Centre Universitaire de Nanterre
2 Rue de Rouen
Nanterre, France

FRENCH GUIANA

Bibliothèque Franconie
97300 Cayenne, F. G.

Musée Local
2 Avenue General de Gaulle
97300 Cayenne, F. G.

GABON

Bibliothèque du Centre d'Information
Libreville, Gabon

Université Nationale du Gabon
B. P. 13
131 Boulevard Leon M'Ba
Libreville, Gabon

GEORGIA

Atlanta Historical Society, Inc.
3099 Andrews Drive, N.W.
Atlanta, GA 30305

Atlanta Public Library, West Hunter Branch
1116 Hunter Street. S.W.
Atlanta, GA 30314

Atlanta University
Trevor Arnett Library
273 Chestnut Street, S.W.
Atlanta, GA 30314

Division of Public Library Services
State Department of Education
156 Trinity Avenue, S.W.
Atlanta, GA 30303
Carlton Thaxton, Director
Telephone: (404) 656-2461

Federal Archives and Records Center
2557 St. Joseph Avenue
East Point, GA 30344
Telephone: (404) 526-7477
(Also serves Alabama, Florida, Kentucky, Mississippi, North
Carolina, South Carolina, and Tennessee.)

Fort Valley State College
Henry Alexander Junt Memorial Library
Fort Valley, GA 31030

Georgia Department of Archives and History
330 Capitol Avenue
Atlanta, GA 30334

Georgia Historical Society
501 Whitaker Street
Savannah, GA 31401

Paine College
Warren A. Chandler Library
Augusta, GA 30901
(Shelf list only, especially race problem as it concerned churches in
the old South.)

Savannah State College Library
Savannah, GA 31404

Vital Records Service
State Department of Public Health
47 Trinity Avenue, S.W.
Atlanta, GA 30334
(Births and deaths 1919.* For records before 1919 in Atlanta or
Savannah, write county health department in area where event
occurred. Marriage records kept since June 9, 1952.)

GHANA

Alliance Française
P. O. Box 1573
Accra, Ghana

Ghana National Museum
Barnes Road
P. O. Box 3343
Accra, Ghana

National Archives of Ghana
P. O. Box 3056
Accra, Ghana

West African Historical Museum
P. O. Box 502
Cape Coast, Ghana

GUADELOUPE

Archives Departementales de la Guadeloupe
B. P. 74
97102 Basse Terre, Guadeloupe

Musée l'Herminier
27 Rue Sadi-Carnet
97111 Pointe-à-Pitre, Guadeloupe

GUAM

Nieves M. Flores Memorial Library
P. O. Box 652
Agana, GU 96910
Magdalena S. Taitano, Librarian

Office of Vital and Health Statistics
Department of Public Health and Social Services
Government of Guam
P. O. Box 2816
Agana, GU 96910
(Births and deaths, October 26, 1901,* marriages 1899.*)

GUINEA

Archives Nationales
B. P. 561 Bis
Conakry, Guinea

Institut de Recherches et de Documentation
B. P. 561
Conakry, Guinea

Musée National
Conakry, Guinea

GUYANA

Museum
Cultural Centre
North Street
Georgetown, Guyana

National Library
P. O. Box 110
Georgetown, Guyana

HAITI

Centre de Documentation
Port au Prince, Haiti

Bibliothèque Nationale d'Haiti
Rue Hammerton Killick
Port au Prince, Haiti

Institut d'Ethnologie d'Haiti
Rue Capois
Port au Prince, Haiti

Institut Haitiano-Americain
Champ de Mars
Port au Prince, Haiti

Musée National
Turgeau, C. S.
Port au Prince, Haiti

Université de L'Etat d'Haiti
Place des Heros de L'Independence
Port au Prince, Haiti

HAWAII

Division of Library Services
P. O. Box 2360
Honolulu, HI 96804
May C. Chun
Telephone: (808) 548-2430

State Department of Health
Research and Statistics Office
P. O. Box 3378
Honolulu, HI 96801
(Births, 1850,* deaths 1861,* marriages 1849.*)

HONDURAS

Asociación de Bibliotecarios y Archivistas de Honduras
11 a Ca
e, Primera y Segunda Avyenidas, No. 105
Comayaguela, D.C.
Tegucigalpa, Honduras

IDAHO

Idaho State Library
325 W. State Street
Boise, ID 83702
Helen M. Miller, State Librarian
Telephone: (208) 384-2150

State Department of Health
Bureau of Vital Statistics
Boise, ID 83707
(Births, deaths, marriages 1911.* Marriage records are in custody of
county recorder for each county.)

ILLINOIS

Department of Public Health
Bureau of Vital Records
525 W. Jefferson Street
Springfield, IL 62706
(Births and deaths 1916.* Marriage records are in custody of each
county clerk from date of county's organization.)

Chicago Board of Health
Room CL
111 Civic Center
50 W. Washington Street
Chicago, IL 60602
(Chicago records 1955.*)

Peoria City Health Department
2116 N. Sheridan Road
Peoria, IL 61604
(Births 1878,* deaths 1872.*)

Federal Archives and Records Center
7358 S. Pulaski Road
Chicago, IL 60629
Telephone: (312) 353-8541
(Also serves Indiana, Michigan, Minnesota, Ohio, and Wisconsin.)

Illinois State Archives
Archives Building
Springfield, IL 62706

Illinois State Historical Library
Old State Capitol
Springfield, IL 62706

Illinois State Historical Society
Old State Capitol
Springfield, IL 62706

Illinois State Library
Centennial Memorial Building
Springfield, IL 62706
Kathryn Gesterfield, Director
Telephone: (217) 525-2994

Museum of African American History
Du Sable Museum of African American History
3806 S. Michigan Avenue
Chicago, IL 60653

Museum of Negro History and Art
3806 S. Michigan Avenue
Chicago, IL 60653

Northwestern University Library
1937 Sheridan Road
Evanston, IL 60201

INDIANA

Division of Vital Records
State Board of Health
1330 W. Michigan Street
Indianapolis, IN 46206
(Births October 1907,* deaths 1900,* marriages 1958.* For birth and
death records from 1882 to 1908, write to county clerk of each county
or check with the state library, Indianapolis. Early marriage records
are in custody of each county clerk from date of organization of
county.)

Indiana State Library
126 N. Senate Avenue
Indianapolis, IN 46204

Gary City Board of Health
Vital Records Department
1429 Virginia Street
Gary, IN 46407
(Lake County clerk has records from 1882 to 1908.)

Indiana Historical Bureau
State Library and Historical Building
Indianapolis, IN 46204

Indiana Historical Society
140 N. Senate Avenue
Indianapolis, IN 46204

Indiana State Library
140 N. Senate Avenue
Indianapolis, IN 46204
Marcelle K. Foote, Director
Telephone: (317) 633-5441

IOWA

Division of Records and Statistics
State Department of Health
Des Moines, IA 50319
(Births 1880,* deaths 1896,* marriages 1916.* Although records exist

for all three since 1880, searches will be made only for the periods
since the dates given above. Marriage records are in probate court
for each county and date back to the organization of the county.)

Iowa State Department of History and Archives
E. 12th Street and Grand Avenue
Des Moines, IA 50319

Traveling Library
Historical Building
Des Moines, IA 50319
Barry Porter, Director
Telephone: (515) 281-5237

IVORY COAST

Archives Nationales
B. P. 1717
Abidjan, Ivory Coast

Bibliothèque Centrale de la Côte d'Ivoire
B. P. 6243
Abidjan-Treichville, Ivory Coast

Bibliothèque de l'Université d'Abidjan
B. P. 8859
Abidjan, Ivory Coast

Bibliothèque du Service d'Information
B. P. 1879
Abidjan, Ivory Coast

JAMAICA

Institute of Jamaica
12–16 East Street
Kingston, Jamaica

Jamaica Archives
Spanish Town
Jamaica Library Service
P. O. Box 58
2 Tom Redcam Drive
Kingston 5, Jamaica   /

University of the West Indies Library
Mona
St. Andrews, Jamaica

KANSAS

Kansas State Library
535 Kansas Avenue
Topeka, KS 66601
Ernestine Gilliland
Telephone: (913) 296-3259

State Department of Health
Division of Vital Statistics
Records Section
Topeka, KS 66612
(Births and deaths 1911,* marriages 1913.*)

City Hall
6th and Ann Streets
Kansas City, KS 66101
City Clerk

Wichita Historical Museum Association
3751 E. Douglas
Wichita, KS 67218

KENTUCKY

Department of Libraries
P. O. Box 537
Frankfort, KY 40601
Charles Hinds, State Librarian
Telephone: (502) 564-4346

Kentucky Historical Society
P. O. Box H
Frankfort, KY 40601

Office of Vital Statistics
State Department of Health
275 E. Main Street
Frankfort, KY 40601
(Births and deaths 1911,* marriages 1958.* Earlier marriages, dating
from organization of county, can be found with each county clerk.)

KENYA

The British Council
Kenya Cultural Centre
P. O. Box 40751
Harry Thuku Road
Nairobi, Kenya

British Institute in Eastern Africa
P. O. Box 30710
Nairobi, Kenya

Historical Association of Kenya
P. O. Box 27027
Nairobi, Kenya

LIBERIA

Government Public Library
Ashmun Street
Monrovia, Liberia

Liberian Information Service Library
Monrovia, Liberia

University of Liberia Libraries
University of Liberia
P. O. Box 9020
Monrovia, Liberia

LIBYA

Archives
Castello
Tripoli, Libya

Ministry of Information and Guidance Libraries
c/o Maidan ash-Shuhada
Tripoli, Libya

University of Libya Library
Banghazi, Libya

LOUISIANA

Dillard University Library
Amistad Research Center
2601 Gentilly Boulevard
New Orleans, LA 70122
(Card index on blacks in New Orleans from newspapers covering the
period 1850–65. The center also contains the records of the American
and Foreign Anti-Slavery Society, American Home Missionary
Society Archives, and the American Missionary Association
Archives.)

Ark-La-Tex Genealogical Association (ALTGA)
P. O. Box 4462
Shreveport, LA 71104
Ms. Barbara Gilbert Smith, Corresponding Secretary
Telephone: (318) 742-1349
(Organization of genealogists interested in southern research,
especially Arkansas, Louisiana, and Texas. Collects and provides
genealogical materials. Supports Genealogy Room of the Shreve
Memorial Library in Shreveport.)

Division of Public Health Statistics
State Department of Health
P. O. Box 60630
New Orleans, LA 70610
(Births and deaths 1914* for the entire state except the city of
New Orleans. Marriage records are in local parishes [counties] in
custody of clerk of court.)

Bureau of Vital Statistics
New Orleans City Health Department
1 WO 3 City Hall
Civic Center
New Orleans, LA 70112
(Births 1790,* deaths 1804,* marriages 1831.*)

Grambling College of Louisiana
A. C. Memorial Library
P. O. Box 3
Grambling, LA 71245

Louisiana Historical Association
P. O. Box 44422
Capitol Station
Baton Rouge, LA 70804

Louisiana Historical Society
630 Maison Blanche Building
921 Canal Street
New Orleans, LA 70112

Louisiana State Library
P. O. Box 131
Baton Rouge, LA 70800
Thomas Jaques
Telephone: (504) 389-6651

Louisiana State University and Agricultural and Mechanical College
   Library
Baton Rouge, LA 70803

Xavier University Library
Palmetto and Pine Streets
New Orleans, LA 70125

MALAGASY REPUBLIC (MADAGASCAR)

Archives Nationales
B. P. 3384
Tananarive, M. R.

Bibliothèque Nationale
Antaninarenina
B. P. 257
Tananarive, M. R.

Office de la Recherche Scientifique et Technique Outre-Mer
Centre de Tananarive
B. P. 434
Tananarive, M. R.

MAINE

Maine Historical Society
485 Congress Street
Portland, ME 04111

Maine State Archives
State Archivist
State House
Augusta, ME 04330

Maine State Museum Commission
State House
Augusta, ME 04330

Office of Vital Statistics
State Department of Health and Welfare
State House
Augusta, ME 04330
(Births, deaths, marriages 1892.* Earlier records may be found in
files of town clerk of town where event occurred.)

Maine State Library
Augusta, ME 04330
Gary Nichols, State Librarian
Telephone: (207) 289-3561

MALI

Archives Nationales du Mali
Institut des Sciences Humaines
Koulouba
Bamako, Mali

Bibliothèque Nationale
Institut des Sciences Humaines
Koulouba
Bamako, Mali

Centre de Documentation et de Recherches Historiques "Ahmen
  Baba" (CEDRAB)
B. P. 14
Timbuktu, Mali

MARTINIQUE

Archives Departementales de la Martinique
B. P. 720 Boulevard du Chevalier de Sainte-Marie
97262 Fort de France, Martinique

MARYLAND

Division of Library Development and Services
State Department of Education
P. O. Box 8717
Baltimore, MD 21240
Telephone: (301) 796-8300
Nettie B. Taylor, Assistant State Superintendent for Libraries

Division of Vital Records
State Department of Health
State Office Building
301 W. Preston Street
Baltimore, MD 21201
(Births and deaths, 1898,* marriages June 1951,* for the entire state
except the city of Baltimore.)

Baltimore City Health Department
Bureau of Vital Records
Municipal Office Building
Baltimore, MD 21202

Maryland Hall of Records
Commission Library
P. O. Box 828
College Avenue and St. John's Street
Annapolis, MD 21404
(Very early records.)

Maryland Historical Society
201 W. Monument Street
Baltimore, MD 21201

MASSACHUSETTS

Federal Archives and Records Center
380 Trapelo Road
Waltham, MA 02154
(Also serves Connecticut, Maine, New Hampshire, Rhode Island,
and Vermont.)

Massachusetts Bureau of Library Extension
Department of Education
648 Beacon Street
Boston, MA 02215
Charles R. Joyce, Director
Telephone: (616) 536-4030 or 4031

Massachusetts Historical Society
1154 Boyleston Street
Boston, MA 02215

Massachusetts Historical Commission
Office of the Secretary
State House
Boston, MA 02133

New England Historic Genealogical Society
101 Newbury Street
Boston, MA 02116
Telephone: (617) 536-5740
(Collects materials on family and local history.)

Office of the Secretary of State
Division of Vital Statistics
272 State House
Boston, MA 02133
(Births, deaths, marriages 1841,* for the entire state except the city
of Boston. Earlier records can be found in files of city or town clerk
where event occurred.)

Registry Division
Health Department
Room 705, City Hall Annex
Boston, MA 02133
City Registrar
(Records since 1639.)

MICHIGAN

Association for the Study of Negro Life and History, Detroit Branch
2974 Elmhurst Avenue
Detroit, MI 48206

Historical Society of Michigan
2117 Washtenaw Avenue
Ann Arbor, MI 48104

Detroit Public Library
5201 Woodward
Detroit, Michigan 48202

Michigan State Library
735 E. Michigan Avenue
Lansing, MI 48913
Francis X. Scannell, State Librarian
Telephone: (517) 373-1580

Vital Records Section
Michigan Department of Health
3500 N. Logan Street
Lansing, MI 48914
(Births and deaths 1867,* marriages 1868.*)

City Health Department
3500 North Logan Street
Detroit, MI
(Detroit births 1893,* deaths 1897.*)

MINNESOTA

Library Division
Department of Education
301 Hanover Building
480 Cedar Street
St. Paul, MN 55101
William Asp, Director
Telephone: (612) 296-2821

Minnesota Historical Society
690 Cedar Street
St. Paul, MN 55101

Section of Vital Statistics
State Department of Health
350 State Office Building
St. Paul, MN 55101
(Births and deaths 1900.* Marriage records are in custody of clerk of
the district court in each county.)

Section of Vital Statistics
State Department of Health
717 Delaware Street, S.E.
Minneapolis, MN 55440

MISSISSIPPI

Mississippi Department of Archives and History
War Memorial Building
P. O. Box 571
Jackson, MS 39205
(Many marriage records back to 1826.*)

Mississippi Historical Society
P. O. Box 571
Jackson, MS 39205

Mississippi Library Commission
405 State Office Building
Jackson, MS 39201
Mary Love, Director
Telephone: (601) 354-6369

Tougaloo College
Eastman Library
Tougaloo, MS 39174

Vital Records Registration
State Board of Health
P. O. Box 1700
Jackson, MS 39205
(Births and deaths 1912.* Marriage records 1926* are in custody of
clerk of the circuit court in each county.)

MISSOURI

Federal Archives and Records Center
2306 E. Bannister Road
Kansas City, MO 64131
Telephone: (816) 926-7271
(Also serves Iowa, Kansas, and Nebraska.)

Missouri Historical Society
Jefferson Memorial Building
St. Louis, MO 63112

Missouri State Library
308 E. High Street
State Office Building
Jefferson City, MO 65102
Charles O'Halloran, State Librarian
Telephone: (314) 751-2751

Vital Records
Division of Health
State Department of Public Health and Welfare
Jefferson City, MO 65101
(Births and deaths 1910.* Marriage records are in custody of recorder
of deeds in each county, and many date back to county organization.)

Kansas City Health Department
10th Floor
City Hall
Kansas City, MO 64106

St. Louis Department of Health
Bureau of Vital Statistics
Room 10
Municipal Courts Building
1320 Market Street
St. Louis, MO 63103
(Births 1870,* deaths 1850.*)

MONTANA

Division of Records and Statistics
State Department of Health
Helena, MT 59601
(Births and deaths 1907,* marriages 1943.* Earlier marriage records,
dating from organization of county, are in custody of clerk of court
of each county.)

Montana Historical Society
225 N. Robert Street
Helena, MT 59601

Montana State Library
930 E. Lyndale Avenue
Helena, MT 59601
Alma Jacobs, State Librarian
Telephone: (406) 449-3004

MOROCCO

Bibliothèque Générale et Archives
Avenue Moulay Cherif
Rabat, Morocco

Bibliothèque Municipale
142 Avenue des Forces Armées Royales
Casablanca, Morocco

MOZAMBIQUE

Arquivo Historico de Mocambique
C. P. 2033
Lourenço Marques, Mozambique

Bibliotheca Nacionala de Mocambique
C. P. 141
Lourenço Marques, Mozambique

NEBRASKA

Bureau of Vital Statistics
State Department of Health
P. O. Box 94757
Lincoln, NB 68509
(Births and deaths 1904,* marriages 1909.* Earlier marriage records
are in custody of county judge in each county.)

Omaha-Douglas County Health Department
Division of Vital Statistics
1602 S. 50th Street
Omaha, NB 68106

Nebraska Public Library Commission
Lincoln, NB 68509
Jane P. Geske, Director
Telephone: (402) 471-2045

Nebraska State Historical Society
1500 R Street
Lincoln, NB 68508

NEVADA

Department of Health, Welfare, and Rehabilitation
Division of Health
Section of Vital Statistics
Carson City, NV
Joseph J. Anderson, State Librarian
Telephone: (702) 885-5130

NEW HAMPSHIRE

New Hampshire Historical Society
30 Park Street
Concord, NH 03301

New Hampshire State Historical Commission
71 S. Fruit Street
Concord, NH 03301

New Hampshire State Library
20 Park Street
Concord, NH 03302
Avis Duckworth, Acting State Librarian
Telephone: (603) 271-2392

State Department of Health and Welfare
Bureau of Vital Statistics
61 S. Spring Street
Concord, NH 03301
(Births, deaths, marriages 1640.* Town clerk of each town also has
these vital statistics.)

NEW JERSEY

Federal Archives and Records Center
Building 22-MOT Bayonne
Bayonne, NJ 07002
(Also serves New York, Puerto Rico, and Virgin Islands.)

New Jersey Bureau of Archives and History
State Library
185 W. State Street
Trenton, NJ 08625
Director
Telephone: (609) 292-6200

New Jersey Historical Commission
State Library
185 W. State Street
Trenton, NJ 08625

State Department of Health
Bureau of Vital Statistics
P. O. Box 1540
Trenton, NJ 08625
(Births, deaths, marriages 1878.* The records from May 1848 through
May 1878 are in the State Library. Some records of 1665 to 1880 are
in Vol. 22, New Jersey Archives, Series 1.)

Camden City Department of Health
Bureau of Vital Statistics
Room 103
City Hall
Camden, NJ 08101
(Camden records 1924.*)

Elizabeth City Department of Health
Bureau of Vital Statistics
City Hall
Elizabeth, NJ 07202
(Elizabeth records 1848.*)

Newark City Division of Health
Bureau of Vital Statistics
City Hall
Newark, NJ 07102
(Newark records 1850.*)

Paterson City Board of Health
25 Mill Street
Paterson, NJ 07501
(Paterson records 1902* and 1910.*)

NEW MEXICO

Historical Society of New Mexico
P. O. Box 1442
Socorro, NM 87801

State Department of Health and Social Services
P. O. Box 2348
Santa Fe, NM 87501
(Births and deaths 1920.* Write county clerk of each county for
marriage records.)

New Mexico State Library
300 Don Gaspar Street
Santa Fe, NM 87501
C. Edwin Dowlin, State Librarian
Telephone: (505) 827-2103

NEW YORK

Bureau of Vital Statistics
State Department of Health
84 Holland Avenue
Albany, NY 12208
(Births, deaths, marriages 1880,* except for New York City, Albany,
Buffalo, and Yonkers.)

Bronx District Health Center
1826 Arthur Avenue
Bronx, NY 10457

Kings County Historical Division
360 Adams Street
Brooklyn, NY 11201
County clerk
(Brooklyn records from 1847 to 1865.)

Bureau of Records and Statistics
Department of Health of New York City
295 Flatbush Avenue Extension
Brooklyn, NY 11210
(Brooklyn records since 1866.)

Manhattan District Health Center
125 Worth Street
New York City, NY 10013

Municipal Archives and Records Retention Center
New York Public Library
238 William Street
New York City, NY 10038
(Records from 1847 to 1865)

Queens District Health Center
90-37 Parsons Boulevard
Jamaica, Queens, NY 11432
(Records before 1898 are in Albany.)

Office of City Clerk
88-11 Sutphin Boulevard
Jamaica, Queens, NY 11435
(Queens marriage records.)

Richmond District Health Center
55-61 Stuyvesant Place
St. George, Staten Island, NY 10301
(Records before 1898 are in Albany.)

Albany City Health Department
City Hall
Albany, NY 12207
Registrar of Vital Statistics
(Albany records 1870.*)

Buffalo City Health Department
Room 613
City Hall
Buffalo, NY 14202
Registrar of Vital Statistics

Yonkers City Department of Public Health
Bureau of Vital Statistics
Yonkers, NY 10701

Columbia University Libraries
Alexander Gumby Collection
Special Collections Department
New York City, NY 10027

Division of Library Development
New York State Library
State Department of Education
Albany, NY 12201
Robert Flores, Acting Director
Telephone: (518) 474-4969

National Association for the Advancement of Colored People
20 W. 40th Street
New York City, NY 10018

Native New Yorkers Historical Association
503 W. 22nd Street
New York City, NY 10011

New York Genealogical and Biographical Society (NYGBS)
122 E. 58th Street
New York City, NY 10022
Marie F. Berry, Executive Secretary
Telephone: (212) 755-8532
(Procures and preserves materials relating to genealogy, biography,

and family history. Maintains research library of 55,000 volumes.
Publishes church records in New York and adjacent states, manuscript
genealogies, and family Bible records. Maintains microfilm division.)

New York Public Library
Fifth Avenue
New York, NY 10036

New York Public Library
Harlem Branch
Schomburg Collection
103 W. 135th Street
New York City, NY 10030
(A library of books, periodicals, manuscripts, clippings, pictures,
prints, records, sheet music, attempting to record the entire experience
of peoples of African descent—historical and contemporary.
Restricted use; materials must be used on premises.)

New York State Historical Association
P. O. Box 391
Cooperstown, NY 13326

NIGER

Archives de la Republique du Niger
Niamey, Niger

Musée National du Niger
B. P. 248
Niamey, Niger

NIGERIA

Historical Society of Nigeria
c/o Department of History
University of Ife
Ile-Ife, Nigeria

National Archives
P. M. B. 4
University of Ibadan Post Office
Ibadan, Nigeria

National Library of Nigeria
4 Wesley Street
P. M. B. 12626
Lagos, Nigeria

NORTH CAROLINA

Bennett College
Thomas F. Holgate Library
Greensboro, NC 27401

Department of Cultural Resources
Office of State Libraries
109 E. Jones Street
Raleigh, NC 27611
Philip S. Ogilvie, Administrator
Telephone: (919) 829-4129

Duke University
William R. Perkins Library
Durham, NC 27706

North Carolina Literary and Historical Association, Inc.
P. O. Box 1881
Raleigh, NC 27602

North Carolina State Department of Archives and History
109 E. Jones Street
Raleigh, NC 27611

Office of Vital Statistics
State Board of Health
P. O. Box 2091
Raleigh, NC 27602
(Births 1913,* deaths 1906,* marriages 1962.* Marriage records are in
custody of register of deeds in each county. Marriage bonds from
1760 to 1968 have been published.)

Richard B. Harrison Public Library
214 S. Blount Street
Raleigh, NC 27420

University of North Carolina
Louis Round Wilson Library
Chapel Hill, NC 27514

NORTH DAKOTA

State Library Commission
Liberty Memorial Building
Bismarck, ND 58501

Richard Wolfert, Director
Telephone: (701) 224-2490

Division of Vital Statistics
State Department of Health
17th Floor
State Capitol
Bismarck, ND 58501
(Births and deaths 1883,* marriages July 1925.* Earlier marriage
records in custody of county judge in each county.)

State Historical Society of North Dakota
Liberty Memorial Building
Bismarck, ND 58501

OHIO

Afro-American Cultural and Historical Society Historical Museum
8716 Harkness Road
Cleveland, OH 44106

Central State University
Hallie Q. Brown Memorial Library
Wilberforce, OH 45384

Division of Vital Statistics
State Department of Health
65 S. Front Street
G-20 State Department Building
Columbus, OH 43215
(Births and deaths 1908,* marriages 1949.* For records before these dates, write to probate court in county where event occurred.)

Cleveland City Health Department
Bureau of Vital Statistics
Room 18
City Hall
Cleveland, OH 44114
(Cleveland births and deaths 1878,* marriages 1880.*)

Probate Court
1230 Ontario Street
Cleveland, OH 44113
(Cleveland marriages before 1880.)

Ohio Historical Society
Ohio Historical Center
Columbus, OH 43211

Ohio State Library
State Office Building
Columbus, OH 43215
Joseph F. Shubert, State Librarian
Telephone: (614) 469-2694

Western Reserve Historical Society
10825 East Boulevard
Cleveland, OH 44106

Wilberforce University
Daniel Alexander Payne Collection
Carnegie Library
Wilberforce, OH 45384

OKLAHOMA

Division of Vital Statistics
State Department of Health
3400 N. Eastern Avenue
Oklahoma City, OK 73105
(Births and deaths 1908.* Marriage records are filed at the courthouse
in each county.)

Oklahoma Department of Libraries
200 18th Street, N.E.
P. O. Box 53344
Oklahoma City, OK 73105
Ralph H. Funk, Director
Telephone: (405) 521-2502

Oklahoma Historical Society
Historical Building
Oklahoma City, OK 73105

OREGON

Oregon Historical Society
1230 W. Park Avenue
Portland, OR 97205

Oregon State Library
Salem, OR 97310
Eloise Ebert, State Librarian
Telephone: (503) 378-4367

Vital Statistics Section
State Board of Health
P. O. Box 231
Portland, OR 97207
(Births and deaths 1903,* marriages 1907.* Marriage records 1845*
are in custody of county clerk of each county.)

PENNSYLVANIA

Division of Vital Statistics
State Department of Health
P. O. Box 90
Harrisburg, PA 17120
(Births and deaths 1906.* Records from 1852 to 1859 are in custody
of register of wills in each county. Marriages before 1790 are published
in Vol. 2 of Pennsylvania Archives, Series 2.)

Allegheny County Health Department
Division of Vital Statistics
Room 637
City County Building
Pittsburgh, PA 15219
(Pittsburgh records from 1870 to 1905. Records after 1905 are in
Harrisburg.)

Vital Statistics
Philadelphia Department of Public Health
City Hall Annex
Philadelphia, PA 19107
(Philadelphia records from 1860 to 1915.)

Federal Archives and Records Center
5000 Wissahickon Avenue
Philadelphia, PA 19144
Telephone: (215) 438-5200, extension 591
(Also serves Delaware. For the loan of microfilm, also serves District
of Columbia, Maryland, Virginia, West Virginia.)

The Free Library of Philadelphia
Afro-American Collection
Social Science and History Department
Logan Square
Philadelphia, PA 19103

Genealogical Society of Pennsylvania (GSP)
1300 Locust Street
Philadelphia, PA 19107
Robert E. Putney, Jr., Secretary
Telephone: (215) 545-0391
(Collects historical and genealogical records. Offers courses of study
in particular areas of genealogical research. Maintains library of 3,000
volumes plus extensive microfilm collection.)

Historical Society of Pennsylvania
1300 Locust Street
Philadelphia, PA 19107

Library Company of Philadelphia
1314 Locust Street
Philadelphia, PA 19107

Lincoln University
Langston Hughes Memorial Library
Lincoln University, PA 19352

Pennsylvania Historical and Museum Commission
P. O. Box 1026
Harrisburg, PA 17108

Pennsylvania State Library
P. O. Box 1601
Walnut Street and Commonwealth Avenue
Harrisburg, PA 17126
Ernest E. Doerschuk, Jr., State Librarian
Telephone: (717) 787-2646

PUERTO RICO

Archivo General de Puerto Rico
Instituto de Cultura Puertorriquena
San Juan, PR

Caribbean Regional Library
Ponce de Leon
Hato Rey, PR 00919

Public Library Division
Department of Education
Hata Rey, PR 00911
Thilda Alverado, Director
Telephone: (809) 764-6471

RÉUNION

Association Historique Internationale de l'Ocean Indien
B. P. 349
97400 Saint-Denis, Réunion

RHODE ISLAND

Brown University
John Hay Library
Providence, RI 02912

Department of State Library Services
95 Davis Street
Providence, RI 02908
Jewel Drickamer, Director
Telephone: (401) 277-2726

Division of Vital Statistics
State Department of Health
Room 351
State Office Building
101 Smith Street
Providence, RI 02903
(Births, deaths, marriages 1853.* For records before that date, write
to town clerk in town where event occurred. Records from 1636 have
been published and arranged alphabetically by town and event in the
James N. Arnold Collection of Rhode Island Vital Records.)

Newport Historical Society Library
82 Touro Street
Newport, RI 02840

Providence Public Library
150 Empire Street
Providence, RI 02903

The Rhode Island Historical Society
52 Power Street
Providence, RI 02906

SENEGAL

Archives de Senegal
Avenue Roume
Dakar, Senegal

Bibliothèque de l'Université de Dakar
B. P. 2006
Dakar, Senegal

Institut Fondamental d'Afrique Noire
Université de Dakar
B. P. 206
Dakar, Senegal

SIERRA LEONE

Public Archives of Sierra Leone
c/o Fourah Bay College Library
P. O. Box 87
Freetown, S. L.

Sierra Leone Society
c/o Department of Modern History
University of Sierra Leone
Freetown, Sierra Leone

SOUTH CAROLINA

Benedict College
Starks Library
Taylor and Harden Streets
Columbia, SC 29204

Bureau of Vital Statistics
State Board of Health
J. Marion Sims Building
Columbia, SC 29210
(Births and deaths 1915,* marriages 1950.* There are few records
before Civil War period. Charleston County Health Department
records Charleston births 1877,* deaths 1821.*)

Miriam B. Wilson Foundation
The Old Slave Mart Museum
6 Chalmers Street
Charleston, SC 29401

South Carolina Historical Society
Chalmers and Meeting Streets
Charleston, SC 29401

South Carolina Department of Archives and History
1430 Senate Street
Columbia, SC 29211

South Carolina State Library
1500 Senate Street
P. O. Box 11469
Columbia, SC 29201
Estellene P. Walker
Telephone: (803) 758-3181 or 3182

SOUTH DAKOTA

Division of Public Health Statistics
State Department of Health
Pierre, SD 57501
(Births, deaths, marriages 1906.* Marriage records before that date
are in custody of clerk of the circuit court at county seat.)

South Dakota State Historical Society
Soldiers' and Sailors' Memorial Building
Pierre, SD 57501

South Dakota State Library Commission
322 S. Fort Street
Pierre, SD 57501
Herschel V. Anderson, Director
Telephone: (605) 224-3131

SPAIN

Archiva Historico Nacional
Calle Serrano
Madrid, Spain

Biblioteca, Archivo y Documentación de Africa
Dirección General de Promocion de Sahara
Paseo de la Castellana
Madrid, Spain

Biblioteca Nacional
Avenida de Cal. V. O. Sotelo
Madrid, Spain

Real Biblioteca de San Lorenzo de El Escorial
El Escorial, Spain

TENNESSEE

Division of Vital Statistics
State Department of Public Health
Cordell Hull Building
Nashville, TN 37219
(Births and deaths 1914.* At the same address are birth records for
Nashville 1881,* Knoxville 1881,* Chattanooga 1882,* and death
records for Nashville 1872,* Knoxville 1887,* Chattanooga 1872.*
Marriage records before 1945 are in custody of county clerk in each
county.)

Fisk University Library
Nashville, TN 37203
(Manuscripts—restricted use, noncirculating.)

Tennessee Historical Society
200 State Library and Archives Building
Nashville, TN 37219

Tennessee State Library and Archives
403 7th Avenue, N.
Nashville, TN 37219
Katheryn C. Culbertson, State Librarian and Archivist
Telephone: (615) 741-2451

TEXAS

Bureau of Vital Statistics
State Department of Health
410 E. 5th Street
Austin, TX 78701
(Births and deaths 1903.* Marriages before 1966 are in custody of
county clerk of county where license was issued.)

San Antonio Metropolitan Health District
131 W. Nueva Street
San Antonio, TX 78204
(San Antonio births 1897,* deaths 1873.*)

Federal Archives and Records Center
4900 Hemphill Street (building address)
P. O. Box 6216 (mailing address)
Fort Worth, TX 76115
Telephone: (817) 334-5515
(Also serves Arkansas, Louisiana, New Mexico, and Oklahoma.)

Texas Library and Historical Commission
1201 Brazos Street
P. O. Box 12927
Capitol Station
Austin, TX 78711

Texas Southern University Library
3201 Wheeler Street
Houston, TX 77004
(Maps, photographs.)

Texas State Historical Association
Sid Richardson Hall 2/306
University Station
Austin, TX 78712

Texas State Library
P. O. Box 12927
Capitol Station
Austin, TX 78711
Dr. Dorman H. Winfrey, Director-Librarian
Telephone: (512) 475-2166

University of Texas at Austin Library
Austin, TX 78712

TRUST TERRITORY OF THE PACIFIC ISLANDS

Department of Education
Saipan, Marianas 96950
Daniel J. Peacock, Supervisor of Library Services

VERMONT

Department of Libraries
State of Vermont
Montpelier, VT 05601
John McCrossan, Commissioner
Telephone: (802) 828-3261

Vermont Historical Society
Pavilion Building
Montpelier, VT 05602

Vital Records Department
Office of Secretary of State
State House
Montpelier, VT 05602
(Birth and death records are in custody of town or city clerk where
event occurred. Births 1760,* deaths 1857,* marriages 1780.*)

VIRGIN ISLANDS

Department of Conservation and Cultural Affairs
Government of the Virgin Islands
P. O. Box 599
Charlotte Amalie, St. Thomas, VI 00810
Director of Libraries and Museum

Department of Health
Bureau of Vital Records
Charlotte Amalie, St. Thomas, VI 00802
(Births and deaths 1906,* marriages 1954.* Clerk of the district court
at St. Thomas has marriage records.)

VIRGINIA

Bureau of Vital Records and Statistics
State Department of Health
James Madison Building
P. O. Box 1000
Richmond, VA 23208
(Births and deaths 1912,* marriages 1853.* There are also some birth
and death records for 1853 to 1896. The county clerk in each county
has marriage records before 1853. Some cities had vital records before
the state: Roanoke 1891,* Norfolk 1892,* Newport News 1896,*
Portsmouth 1900,* Richmond 1900,* Lynchburg 1910,*
Petersburg 1900,* and Elizabeth City County 1900.*)

College of William and Mary
Earl Gregg Swem Library
Williamsburg, VA 23185

Hampton Institute
George Foster Peabody Collection
The Collis P. Huntington Memorial Library
Hampton, VA 23668

University of Virginia
Alderman Library, Manuscript Division
Charlottesville, VA 22901

Virginia Historical Society
428 North Boulevard
Richmond, VA 23221

Virginia State College Library
Norfolk Division
2401 Corprew Avenue
Norfolk, VA 23504

Virginia State Library
12th and Capitol Streets
Richmond, VA 23219
Donald R. Haynes, State Librarian
Telephone: (804) 770-3338

Virginia Union University
William J. Clark Library
1500 Lombardy Street
Richmond, VA 23173

WASHINGTON

Bureau of Vital Statistics
State Department of Health
Public Health Building
Olympia, WA 98501
(Births and deaths July 1907,* marriages 1968.* Marriage records
before that date are in custody of county auditor in each county, as
well as other earlier records.)

Spokane City Health Department
Vital Statistics
Room 551
City Hall
Spokane, WA 99201
(Spokane records 1891.*)

Tacoma-Pierce County Health Department
Room 654
County-City Building
Tacoma, WA 98402
(Tacoma births and deaths 1887,* marriages 1861.*)

Federal Archives and Records Center
6125 Sand Point Way, N.E.
Seattle, WA 98115
Telephone: (206) 442-4502
(Also serves Alaska, Idaho, and Oregon.)

Washington State Historical Society
315 N. Stadium Way
Tacoma, WA 98403

Washington State Library
Olympia, WA 98501
Roderick Swartz, State Librarian
Telephone: (206) 753-5592

WEST VIRGINIA

Division of Vital Statistics
State Department of Health
State Office Building No. 3
Charleston, WV 25305
(Births and deaths 1917,* marriages 1921.* Some records are in
custody of county clerk in each county.)

Library Commission
2004 Quarrier Street
Charleston, WV 25311
Frederic J. Glazer, Executive Secretary
Telephone: (304) 348-2041

West Virginia Department of Archives and History
400 E. Wing, State Capitol
Charleston, WV 25305

West Virginia Historical Society
400 E. Wing, State Capitol
Charleston, WV 25305

WISCONSIN

Bureau of Health Statistics
Wisconsin Division of Health
P. O. Box 309
Madison, WI 53701
(Births and deaths 1876,* marriages 1840.* Some records go back to
1814. Marriage records are in custody of county clerk and of recorder
of deeds in some counties.)

Division of Library Services
Wisconsin Department of Public Instruction
Wisconsin Hall
126 Langdon Street
Madison, WI 53703
W. Lyle Eberhart, Administrator
Telephone: (608) 266-2205

State Historical Society of Wisconsin
816 State Street
Madison, WI 53706

WYOMING

Division of Vital Statistics
State Department of Health
State Office Building
Cheyenne WY 82001
(Births and deaths 1909,* marriages 1914.* Earlier marriage records
are in custody of county clerk of each county.)

Wyoming State Archives and Historical Department
State Office Building
Cheyenne, WY 82001

Wyoming State Library
Supreme Court Building
Cheyenne, WY 82001
William H. Williams, State Librarian
Telephone: (307) 777-7281

Appendix B

NEWSPAPERS

Although many of the newspapers below are out of print, they provide the information that should be helpful for those tracing genealogy: beneficial societies, petition signers, birth dates of members of the community, the names of blacks who participated in the Civil War and wars that followed, members of political conventions, members of church communities, members of fraternal organizations such as the Odd Fellows, the Masons, Daughters of Isis, and the Elks.

Good resources for information on black newspapers:

1. *The Afro-American Press and Its Editors*, by Penn I. Garland. New York: Arno Press, 1969.
   Reviews black magazines and newspapers published between 1827 and 1891.
2. *Encyclopedic Directory of Ethnic Newspapers and Periodicals in the United States*, by Lubomyr R. Wynar. Littleton, Colo.: Libraries Unlimited, 1972.
   Forty-three ethnic groups are represented in this directory of over 900 ethnic newspapers. Titles are arranged alphabetically, addresses are included.
3. *The Black Press Periodical Directory—1975*. Afram Associates, Inc., 68–72 East 131st Street, New York, New York, 10037.

Inquire at the nearest public library and check with the reference librarian—ask for a directory of out-of-print newspapers in their location, or write to the state library or state archives, the Library of Congress, Washington, D.C., and the National Archives, Washington, D.C. In some instances, there are only one or two copies for some of these newspapers, and they might be kept in a special place in the library; however, most are now on microfilm.

I. Early Colonial Newspapers
That Published Slave Advertisements

Boston Independent Advertiser
Connecticut Gazette

Connecticut Journal and New Haven Post Boy
Delaware Courant and Weekly Advertiser
Delaware Gazette
The Georgia Gazette or Independent Register
The Guardian of Freedom, Frankfort Kentucky
The Kentuky Gazette
Maryland Gazette
Maryland Journal and Baltimore Advertiser
Massachusetts Spy
Missouri Gazette
Missouri Republican
Mobile Gazette
The New England Journal
New Hampshire Gazette Portsmouth
The New Jersey Gazette
The New Jersey Journal
New Orleans Advertiser and Prices Current
New York Gazette
New York Weekly Journal
New York Weekly Post Boy
The Norfolk Intelligencer
North Carolina Gazette
Orleans Gazette
The Pennsylvania Chronical and Universal Advertiser
Pennsylvania Gazette
Pennsylvania Journal
Virginia Gazette
Virginia Gazette, Williamsburg, Virginia

II. Out of Print Newspapers whose issues can be traced. Dates in parentheses indicate first year of issue.

The Christian Recorder (1856), Philadelphia, Pennsylvania
Colored American (1837), New York, New York
Colored Tennessean (1866)
Elevator (1842), San Francisco, California
Freedom's Journal (1827), New York, New York
Guardian (1901), Boston, Massachusetts
Impartial Citizen (1848), Syracuse, New York

Indianapolis Freeman (1888), Indianapolis, Indiana
Loyal Georgian (1865), Augusta, Georgia
The Mirror of Liberty (1837), New York, New York
The Mystery (1843), Pittsburgh, Pennsylvania
The National Reformer (1833), New York, New York
New Orleans Louisianian (1866), New Orleans, Louisiana
New York Age (1907), New York, New York
The North Star and The Douglas Paper (1847), Rochester,
    New York
Our National Progress, Wilmington, Delaware
The Palladium of Liberty (1844), Columbus, Ohio
The Ram's Horn (1847), New York, New York
Rights of All (1829), New York, New York
The Star of Zion (1867), Charlotte, North Carolina
Western Sentinel of Kansas City, Kansas City, Kansas

III. Current Newspapers *The following newspapers have a long
    history and are still publishing. (Dates in parentheses
    indicate first year of issue.)*

Afro-American (1892), Baltimore, Maryland
Amsterdam News (1909), Harlem, New York City,
    New York
Chicago Defender (1905), Chicago, Illinois
Norfolk Journal and Guide (1910), Norfolk, Virginia
Philadelphia Tribune (1884), Philadelphia, Pennsylvania
Pittsburgh Courier (1910), Pittsburgh, Pennsylvania
Spokesman and Recorder (1934), Minneapolis, Minnesota

BIBLIOGRAPHY

Abajian, James de T., *Blacks in Selected Newspapers, Censuses and Other Sources; An Index to Names and Subjects.* Boston: G. K. Hall and Co., 1976. The text identifies and cites references to individual blacks in black newspapers and periodicals in the United States. An excellent publication for those interested in tracing black genealogy, this text provides personal names and activities, and is a guide to the wide variety of published sources of the nineteenth and early twentieth centuries, with over 90,000 entries.

Afro-American 1553–1906. Author Catalog of the Library Co. of Philadelphia and the Historical Society of Pennsylvania. Boston: G. K. Hall and Co., 1973. Excellent research material consisting of the collection of two of the most prestigious archives in the nation.

Allen, Richard, *The Life, Experience and Gospel Labor of the Rt. Rev. Richard Allen.* Philadelphia, 1830.

"Anna Murray Douglass, My Mother as I Recall Her." *Journal of Negro History*, Vol. 8, pp. 93–98.

Aptheker, Herbert, "Maroons Within the Present Limits of the United States," *The Journal of Negro History.* Vol. 24, No. 2 (April 1939).

Baldwin, James, and Mead, Margaret, *A Rap on Race.* Philadelphia: J. B. Lippincott, 1971.

Barr, Alwyn, *Black Texans. A History of Negroes in Texas.* Austin, Tex.: Jenkins Publishing Company, 1973.

Bassett, John Spencer, *Slavery in the State of North Carolina.* Baltimore: Johns Hopkins Press, 1898.

Beasley, Delilah L., *The Negro Trail Blazer of California.* Los Angeles: 1919.

—"The Beams Family: Free Blacks in Indian Territory." *Journal of Negro History*, Vol. XLI No. 1 (January 1976).

Bedini, Silvio A., *The Life of Benjamin Banneker.* New York: Scribner's Sons, 1972.

Berry, Brewton, *Almost White.* New York: Macmillan Co., 1963.

Biographical Directory of Negro Ministers. Compiled by Ethel L. Williams. Boston: G. K. Hall and Co., 1975.

In Black and White: Afro-America in Present, expanded and revised. Kalamazoo, Mich.: 1975. An alphabetical list of 7,392 names of African and American men and women who have contributed in some way to American life.

Black Names in America: Origins and Usage. Collected by Newbell Niles Puckett, edited by Murray Heller. Boston: G. K. Hall and Co., 1975.

Blassingame, John W., *The Slave Community; Plantation Life in the Ante-Bellum South*. Oxford University Press, 1972.

Blockson, Charles L., *Pennsylvania's Black History*. Philadelphia: Portfolio Associates. 1975.

Bond, Horace M. "Two Racial Islands in Alabama." *American Journal of Sociology*, Vol. 36. Washington, D.C.: Associated Publishers, 1939.

Botkin, B. A., "The Slave As His Own Interpreter." *Quarterly Journal*. Vol. 2., No. 1. (July-August-September 1944).

Brackett, Jefrey R., *The Negro in Maryland: A Study of the Institution of Slavery*. Baltimore: Johns Hopkins University, 1889.

Bruce, Phillip Alexander, *Two Volume Life of John Randolf: A Roanoke*.

Bryk, Felix Voodoo Eros, *Echological Studies in the Sex Life of the African Aboriginies*. New York: United Book Guild, 1964.

Bureau of the Census, Washington D.C. *The Seventh Census of the United States:* Population of the United States in 1850.

Burnell, John P., *The Guineas of West Virginia:* Unpublished M.A. thesis. Ohio State University, 1952.

—"The Bustill Family," *Journal of Negro History*. Vol. X.

Catterall, Helen T. (ed.), *Judicial Cases Concerning American Slavery and the Negro*. Washington, D.C., 1926.

Chanler, David, "The Jackson Whites: An American Episode," *The Crisis*. Vol. 46, No. 5 (May 1930).

Clifton, Lucille, *Generation*. New York: Random House, 1976. Clifton's story focuses on her ancestors from Dahomey.

Cohen, David Steven, *The Ramapo Mountain People*. New Brunswick: Rutgers University Press, 1974. Describes the mixed ancestry of the Jackson Whites.

"Compiled Military Service Records in the National Archives," U.S. Gov't publ. 63-3

Conneau, Theophilus, *A Slaver's Log Book*. Englewood Cliffs, N.J.: Prentice Hall, 1976.

Cox, Samuel S., *Miscegenation or Amalgamation: Fate of the Freedman*. Speech delivered in the House of Representatives, February 17, 1864. Washington, D.C., 1864.

Davis, Russel H., *Black America in Cleveland, 1796-1969*. Cleveland, Ohio: The Associated Publishers, 1972.

Day, Beth, *Sexual Life Between Blacks and Whites*. New York: World Publishing Co., 1972.

Doane, Gilbert Harry, *Searching for Your Ancestors: The How and Why of Genealogy.* Minneapolis: University of Minnesota Press, 1973.

—*Documentary History of American Industrial Society,* "Plantation and Frontier" Cleveland, 1910.

Dodge, Davis, "The Free Negroes of North Carolina." *Atlantic Monthly,* Vol. LVII.

Donald, Henderson H. *The Negro Freedman: Life Conditions of the American Negro in the Early Years After Emancipation.* New York, 1952.

Dover, Cedric, *Half-Caste.* London: Martin, Secker and Warbury Publishers LTD, 1937.

DuBois, W. E. Burghart, *The Negroes of Farmville, Virginia: A Social Study.* United States Department (Bureau] of Labor Bulletin. No. 14. Washington, D.C.

—*The Negro Landholders of Georgia.* United States Department of Labor Bulletin, No. 35. Washington, D.C.

—*The Philadelphia Negro.* Boston: Ginn & Company, 1899.

Emilio, Luis F., *History of the Fifty-Fourth Regiment of Massachusetts Voluntary Infantry, 1863–65.* Boston: The Boston Book Company, 1891.

Envelopes of Sound: Six practitioners discuss the method, theory, and practice of oral history and oral testimony. Edited by Ronald J. Grele. Chicago, 1975.

Fisher, James A. "A History of the Political and Social Development of the Black Community in California, 1859–1950." *Journal of Negro History,* September 1971.

Forten, Charlotte, "Life on the Sea Islands." *Atlantic Monthly,* Vol. 13. (May–June 1864).

Foster, Lawrence, *Negro Indian Relationship in the Southeast.* Philadelphia: University of Pennsylvania Press, 1935.

Frazier, E. Franklin, *Black Bourgeoise.* Glencoe, Illinois: The Free Press, 1957.

—*The Free Negro Family.* Nashville, 1932.

—*The Negro Family in Chicago.* Chicago, 1932.

Freyre, Gilberto, *The Master and the Slaves: A Study in the Development of Brazilian Civilization.* Translated from the Portuguese by Samuel Putman, New York: Alfred A. Knopf Co., 1946.

Frye, Hardy, *Negroes in California from 1841 to 1875.* California

History Series, Monograph, 3, No. 1. San Francisco: Negro
Historical and Cultural Society, April 1968.

"Genealogical Sources Outside the National Archives," U.S. Gov't
publication.

"Genealogical Sources in the National Archives," U.S. Gov't
publ. 62-1

Gilbert, William Harlem Jr., "Surviving Indian Groups of the Eastern
United States," *Smithsonian Report for 1948.* Washington, D.C.:
Government Printing Office, 1949.

Gordon, Taylor, *Born to Be Free.* New York: Covici-Friede, 1929.
Describes the author's life growing up in a black community in
White Sulphur Springs, Montana.

Greene, Lorenzo Johnston, *The Negro in Colonial New England.* New
York: Atheneum, 1969.

Griffin, John Howard, *Black Like Me.* London: Catholic Book Club
Edition, 1960.

*A Guide of the Microfilm Publication of the Papers of the Abolition
Society.* Prepared by Jeffery Nordlinger Bumbrey, published by the
Pennsylvania Abolition Society and the Historical Society of
Pennsylvania, Philadelphia, 1976. The guide provides an excellent
account of the papers of one of the nation's oldest societies
concerned with slavery.

Guide to Genealogical Records in the National Archives (GSA-NA
Pub. 64-8, LC Card #A-64-7048).

Haley, Alex, "Black History, Oral History and Genealogy." *The Oral
History Review,* 1973.

—*Roots,* New York: Doubleday, 1976.

Halsell, Grace, *Black White Sex.* New York: William Morrow and
Company, 1972.

—*Soul Sister.* New York: The World Publishing Co., 1969.

Hancock, Harold B., "Not Quite Men: The Free Negroes in Delaware
in the 1830's." *Civil War History,* Vol. 17 (Dec. 1971).

Harris, Mark, "America's Oldest Interracial Community." *Negro
Digest,* Vol. 6, No. 9 (July 1948).

Harris, M. A., *A Negro History Tour of Manhattan.* New York:
Greenwood Press, 1968.

Henriques, Fernando, *Children of Conflict: A Study of Interracial
Sex and Marriage.* New York, 1975.

Herrick, Cheeseman A., *White Servitude in Pennsylvania.*
Philadelphia, 1926.

Hilborn, Ella. *The History of the Negro Population of Collinwood.* Huron Institute Paper 1: 40-2.

Hilton, Suzanne, *Who Do You Think You Are?* Philadelphia: The Westminister Press, 1976.

Himes, Chester, *The Third Generation.* Cleveland and New York: The World Press, 1954.

"History of the Wilberforce Refugee Colony in Middlesex County." *Transactions* of the London and Middlesex (Ont.) Historical Society, 1919, pt. 9.

Hume, Richard L., *The "Black and Tan" Constitutional Conventions of 1867-1869 in Ten Former Confederate States: A Study of Their Membership.* Microfilm Ph.D. Dissertation, University of Washington, 1969. A-Vrm.

Hurston, Zora Neale, *Dust Tracks on the Road.* Philadelphia: J. B. Lippincott Co. 1942.

Johnson, Charles S., *The Negro in American Civilization.* New York, 1930.

Johnson, James Weldon, *Black Manhattan.* New York, 1930.

—"Documentary Evidence of the Relations of Negroes and Indians." *Journal of Negro History,* Vol. XIV.

Johnston, James Hugo, *Race Relations in Virginia and Miscegenation in the South 1776-1860.* Amherst, Mass.: University of Massachusetts Press, 1970.

Jones, Charles C., *Negro Myths from the Georgia Coast.* New York: Houghton, Mifflin and Co., 1888.

Jones, John L., *History of the Jones Family.* Greenfield, Ohio, 1930.

Jordan, Winthrop D., *White over Black.* Chapel Hill, N.C.: University of North Carolina Press, 1968.

Kemble, Frances Anne, *Journal of a Residence on a Georgian Plantation in 1838-1839.* New York: Harper's and Brothers, 1863.

Kiser, Clyde Veron, *Sea Island to City.* New York: Atheneum, 1969.

—Letter to Dr. Robert E. Park from an investigator in Ohio seeking information concerning the Randolph slaves. *Journal of Negro History.* Vol. VIII. pp. 207-211.

Lewis, Sinclair, *Kingsblood Royal.* New York: Random House, 1947.

Logan, Frenise A., *The Negro in North Carolina 1876-1894.* Chapel Hill, N.C.: University of North Carolina Press, 1964.

Lovell, Caroline Couper, *The Golden Isles of Georgia.* Boston: Little, Brown, and Co., 1932.

Lyton, David, *The Goddamn White Man.* New York: Simon and Schuster, 1961.

Morton, Robert Russa, *Finding a Way Out: an Autobiography.* New York: Doubleday and Page, 1920.

Moss, William W., *Oral History Program Manual.* New York: Praeger, 1974.

Mossell, Aaron A., *The Unconstitutionality of the Laws Against Miscegenation.* Thesis. Philadelphia: University of Pennsylvania School of Law, 1888.

Murray, Alexander L., "The Provincial Freeman: A New Source for the History of the Negro In Canada and the United States." *Journal of Negro History.* Vol. LX, No. 2 (April 1959).

Naske, Claus-M. "Black Blocked by Bureaucracy." *Alaska Journal,* Vol. 1. (Autumn 1971). Provides information on Alaska during the Great Depression.

The Negro in New Jersey. New Jersey Conference of Social Work, 1932.

The Negro in the Reconstruction of Virginia. New Jersey Conference of Social Work, 1926.

"The Negro Migration to Canada after the Fugitive Slave Act of 1850," *Journal of Negro History,* January, 1920.

Bibliography Committee of the New Jersey Library Association, *New Jersey and the Negro. A Bibliography, 1715–1966.* New Jersey Library Association, Trenton: 1967.

Newman, Deborah L., *List of Free Black Heads of Families in the First Census of the United States, 1790.* Washington: National Archives and Record Services, 1973.

Oates, Addison Ford, *The Art of Collecting Genealogy and History.* Tucson: author publication, 1976.

Olmsted, Frederick Law, *A Journey in the Seaboard States in the Year 1853–1854.* New York, 1856. Dix & Edwards Company London

—*A Journey Through Texas: A Saddle Trip on the Southwestern Frontier.* New York: Dix, Edwards and Co., 1857.

—*The Cotton Kingdom: A Traveler's Observations on Cotton and Slavery in the Slave States in the year 1853–1854.* New York, 1861.

—"Organized Negro Communities: A North American Experiment." *Journal of Negro History,* Vol. XLVIII, No. 1, January, 1962.

The Papers of John Marshall. Box 220, Williamsburg, Virginia, 23185

Parker, Elizabeth L., and Abajian, James, *A Walking Tour of the Black Presence in San Francisco During the Nineteenth Century.* San Francisco: San Francisco African American Historical and Cultural Society, 1974.

—"The Passing Tradition and the African Civilization," *Journal of Negro History*, Vol. I, No. 1, (January, 1916).

Paynter, John H., *Fugitive of the Pearl*. Washington, D.C., 1930.

Penn, Irvine G. *The Afro-American Press and Its Editors*. New York, 1969.

"Pension and Bounty—Land Warrant Files in the National Archives," U.S. Gov't publ. 60-9

Phillip, Ulrich B., *American Negro Slavery*. New York, 1927.

Porter, Dorothy, *Early Negro Writing 1760–1837*. Boston: Beacon Press, 1971.

Porter James A., *Modern Negro Art*. New York, 1969.

The Present State of Condition of Free People of Color of the City of Philadelphia and Adjoining Districts as Exhibited by the Report of a Committee of the Pennsylvania Society for Promoting the Abolition of Slaves, Etc. Philadelphia: Nerrew and Gunn, Printers, 1838.

Porter, Kenneth W., "Negroes and the Fur Trade." Reprinted from *Minnesota History*, Vol. 15. (December, 1934).

Purvis, Robert, *Appeal of 40,000 citizens Threatened with Disfranchisement to the People of Pennsylvania*, Philadelphia, 1838. Contains the names of black citizens; original copy of the appeal is located at the Historical Society of Pennsylvania, Philadelphia.

Quarles, Benjamin, "The Colonial Militia and Negro Manpower." *Mississippi Valley Historical Review*. Vol. 45. (March 1959).

"Records in the National Archives Relating to Confederate Soldiers," U.S. Gov't pub. 60-10

Reuter, Edward Buron, *The Mulatto in the United States*. Boston: The Gorham Press, 1918.

Robert Russa Morton of Hampton and Tuskegee. Edited by William Hardin Hughes and Fredrick D. Patterson. Chapel Hill, N.C.: University of North Carolina Press, 1956.

Robeson, Eslanda Goode, *Paul Robeson, Negro*. New York, 1930.

Robeson, Paul, *Here I Stand*. New York, 1958.

Roderick, Thomas H. "Negro Genealogist," *American Genealogist*, March 7, 1971.

Rogers, Joel A., *Nature Knows No Color-Line*. New York, 1952.

—*Sex and Race*. 3 vols., New York, 1940–1944

Roome, William J. Aggrey, *The African Teacher*. London: Marshall, Morgan, and Scott L.T.D. Describes the ancestry of this African-born scholar, who won fame as an educator in America.

Rosengarten, Theodore, *All God's Dangers: The Life of Nate Shaw*. New York: Alfred A. Knopf, 1974.

Roussève, Charles B., *The Negro in Louisiana*. New Orleans: The Xavier University Press, 1937.

Russel, John H., *The Free Negro in Virginia*. Baltimore: Johns Hopkins Press, 1913.

Savage, W. Sherman. "The Negro on the Mining Frontier." Reprinted from The *Journal of Negro History*, Vol. 31. (January 1945).

Scarupa, Harriet Jackson, "Black Genealogy," *Essence* Magazine, July 1976.

Schweninger, Loren, "A Slave Family in the Ante Bellum South." *Journal of Negro History*, Vol. LX, No. 1 (January 1975).

Seibert, Wilbur H. *The Underground Railroad from Slavery to Freedom*. New York, 1898.

Sickls, Robert J. Race. *Marriage and the Law*. Albuquerque: University of New Mexico Press, 1972.

Simmons, William Johnson, *Men of Mark*. Cleveland, 1887. A good biography of prominent black men.

Skalka, Lois Martin, *Tracing, Charting and Writing Your Family History*. New York: Pilot Books, 1975.

Sketches of the Higher Classes of Colored Society in Philadelphia, by a Southerner. Philadelphia, 1841.

Smith, Lillian, *Killers of the Dreams*. New York: W. W. Norton, 1949.

Southern, Eileen, *The Music of Black America: A History*. New York, 1971.

Speck, Frank G. "The Jackson Whites." *Southern Workman*, Vol. 40 No. 7 (February 1911).

Stampp, Kenneth, *The Peculiar Institution*. New York: Alfred A. Knopf, 1965.

Stevens, Walter J., *Chip on My Shoulder*. Boston, 1946. Autobiography of a black man who refused to pass for white.

Steward, William and Theophilus G., *Gouldtown: A Very Remarkable Settlement of Ancient Date*. Philadelphia, 1913.

Still, William, *The Underground Railroad*. Philadelphia, 1872.

Taggart, John H., *Free Military School for Applicants for Command of Colored Troops*. Philadelphia: King and Baird Co., 1864. (Source includes a roster of students.)

Taylor, Alrutheua Ambush, *The Negro of South Carolina During the Reconstruction*. New York, 1969. Originally published in 1924.

Taylor, William, *The Negro of Litwalton, Virginia. A social study of the "Oyster Negro."* United States Department of Labor Bulletin No. 37.

Thomas, David Y., "The Free Negro in Florida Before 1865." *The South Atlantic Quarterly*, Vol. X.

Thomas, W. T., *The Negroes of Sandy Spring, Maryland: A social study*. United States Department of Labor Bulletin No. 32.

Thompson, Mortimer, *What Became of the Slaves on a Georgia Plantation? Great Auction Sale of the Slaves at Savannah, Georgia, March second and third 1859. A Sequel to Mrs. Kemble's Journal.* N.p., 1863.

Thurman, Wallace, *The Blacker the Berry.* New York: The Macaulay Co., 1929.

Torrence, Ridgely. *The Story of John Hope.* New York: The MacMillan Co. 1948.

Turner, Edward Raymond. *The Negro in Pennsylvania.* Washington, 1911.

Turner, Martha Anne, *Yellow Rose of Texas: The Story of a Song.* El Paso, Tex.: Texas Western Press, 1971.

The U.S. Army and the Negro, A Military History Research Collection Bibliography. Special Bibliographic Series Number 2. Carlisle, Pennsylvania: Carlisle Barracks, 1975. This 102-page collection provides an excellent list of books and pamphlets on the question of the black participation in all the United States Wars.)

U.S. War Department. *Names of Enlisted Men Discharged on Account of Brownsville Affray, with Application for Reenlistment: Letter from Acting Secretary of War.* Senate Documents No. 430, 60th Congress, 1st session. Washington D.C. Government Printing Office, 1908.

Voorhis, Harold Van Buren, *Negro Masonry in the United States.* New York, 1949.

Walz, Jay and Audrey, *Bizarre Sisters.* New York, 1950.

Washington, Booker T. *Up from Slavery.* New York: A. L. Burt Co., 1900.

Webb, Frank J. *The Garies and Their Friends.* London: 1857; reprinted by the Arno Press and the New York Times, 1969.

Weslager, C. A., *Delaware's Forgotten Folk: The Story of the Moors and Nanticokes.* Philadelphia: University of Pennsylvania, 1943.

Whiteman, Max, "Black Genealogy," RQ [*Research Quarterly*], Vol. 11, no. 4, 1972. (Whiteman was a pioneer in discussing black genealogy.)

Wierner, Leo, *Africa and the Discovery of America,* 3 volumes. Philadelphia: Innes & Sons, 1920.

Wright, Richard, *Black Boy.* New York: Harper & Brothers, 1937. London, 1921.

Wright, Richard, *Black Boy.* New York: Harper & Brothers 1937

Wright, Richard R., *The Negroes of Xenia, Ohio.* United States Department of Labor Bulletin No. 37.

Index

Mäkeda

Menelik